The Novel and the Modern World

2⁰⁰

D1075832

DAVID DAICHES

The Novel
and the Modern World

REVISED EDITION

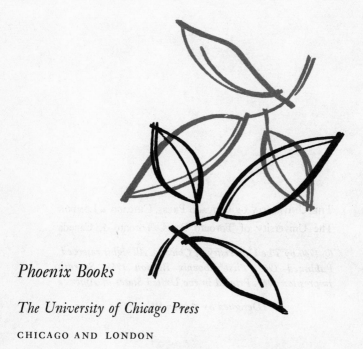

Phoenix Books

The University of Chicago Press

CHICAGO AND LONDON

This book is also available in a clothbound edition from

THE UNIVERSITY OF CHICAGO PRESS

THE UNIVERSITY OF CHICAGO PRESS, CHICAGO & LONDON
The University of Toronto Press, Toronto 5, Canada

© *1960 by The University of Chicago. All rights reserved
Published 1960. First Phoenix Edition 1965. Seventh
Impression 1967. Printed in the United States of America*

Designed by Adrian Wilson

To Billie

Preface

In the twenty-one years that have passed since, very young and very rash, I wrote this book, the modern novel has seen many new developments. But, since my concern was to make a study of a select few of those twentieth-century English novelists who responded most interestingly to the new situation in which the novelist found himself and who in doing so extended the frontiers of their art, I am content to let this second edition remain as a discussion of those heroic pioneers of the earlier part of this century who still dominate the literary scene. Later developments have not challenged the eminence of these pioneers, nor has any novelist of the 1940's or 1950's emulated their achievement. This new edition is not, therefore, simply a bringing-up-to-date of my original book, at least not in the mere chronological sense. It is true that I have added a few words on Virginia Woolf's last novel, which was not written when I first wrote, but on the whole this new edition remains a study of the novel in the first thirty years of the present century.

The main changes that I have made result from shifts in my own point of view. Looking back in 1959—and benefiting, it need hardly be said, by the great volume of criticism that has appeared since I first wrote—I can see clearly that the giants of the modern English novel are Conrad, Joyce, and Lawrence, with Virginia Woolf an important and impressive minor figure whose response to the dilemma of the modern novelist as I understand it is especially interesting. The chapter on Galsworthy, which I included in the first edition, did not really belong to a book on the modern novel in the sense in which I used and still use the term, and I have dropped it. I have omitted also in this edition the chapters on Katherine Mansfield and on Aldous Huxley, not because I consider these writers uninteresting or undistinguished but because they do not really fit into the general scheme of the book and are not in any case "novelists" in the strict sense. I have added two chapters on Lawrence and written an entirely new chapter on Conrad.

I omitted Lawrence in the first edition for the simple reason that I could not quite come to terms with him. I found him both fascinating and frustrating, both a towering genius and an obsessed prophet, and I could not make up my mind about the proper way of approaching him or about the relation between these two aspects. It took me a long time to make up my mind; for some reason, I have resisted coming to terms with Lawrence. But I have done so at last, and I hope the reader will not find the process altogether vain. As for Conrad, it seems to me now that I radically misunderstood what his novels were about. I concentrated on the picturesque Conrad of the Malayan novels and ignored what I now think are his greatest works. The chapter on Conrad in the present edition is thus wholly new and represents my more recent and I hope much more mature views of this novelist, whom I now regard as of the very highest stature.

The opening chapter has also been completely rewritten, though I have not substantially changed the main line of argument. But I have (I hope) sharpened the points and clarified some of the ideas. Looking back now at what I wrote in my middle twenties, I am struck by the confidence with which I pronounced largely on such matters as the nature of civilization and the way in which culture develops. I am much less confident now that I understand the laws of cultural history. In revising those chapters which have not been completely rewritten, I find that I have frequently cut out or modified some rash generalization or substituted for an undocumented assertion a more closely reasoned account of a particular instance. I have also modified some of the political and sociological comment which seemed in the 1930's so necessary and indeed so self-evident, but which now seems to me either irrelevant, because the political situation has changed, or too simple-minded. Yet I have not sacrificed any of the implications of my title; I am still concerned with the novel and the modern world, with the ways in which great novelists responded to certain features of our civilization which emerged about the beginning of the century. I have tried not to write a new book but to rewrite an old one so as to make it correspond more closely to what I now think.

At first I thought that I should rewrite the concluding chapter, which I boldly entitled "Fiction and Civilization." But on reflection I have decided simply to omit it. This is partly because much of that chapter was part of a private quarrel I was having in 1938 with some University of Chicago critics, and both parties to this quarrel have now modified their positions; and partly because I do not feel that any summing-up is necessary. Having sharpened the points made in my opening chapter, and taken greater pains to relate my analyses of particular novels to those points, I think now that any concluding chapter could only be repetitive. Everything I want to say about the way in which these four novelists can be fruitfully related to the culture of their time is said in the individual discussions, and concluding generalizations would but blunt their point.

Finally, I should point out that this book is not intended now, any more than it was twenty-one years ago, as a complete critical study of the novelists discussed. It is meant rather as an illumination of their attitudes and techniques through an investigation of how changed values and changed views about the nature of time and of consciousness have caused new problems and prompted new methods. As I said in my original Foreword: "The following chapters are meant to be neither a history of recent fiction nor a series of individual studies: the relation between the chapters is simply that they are all intended to illustrate, directly or indirectly, the main problems that have faced the writer of fiction in the present century." Perhaps today I would emphasize more the effect on the actual ways of writing novels, and put less stress on illustrating a relationship. But the intention is substantially the same.

                                                        D. D.

JESUS COLLEGE, CAMBRIDGE

Contents

1

Selection
and "Significance"

The changes that came over the English novel in the first half of the twentieth century—changes in technique, in point of view, in the whole relation between the author and his subject—represent something different from the changes to be expected in the development of an established art-form toward greater maturity, greater sophistication, or a more complex handling of the medium, or in its decline into decadence. In the most significant novelists of this period there took place, either implicitly or explicitly, a radical redefinition of the nature and function of fiction. The English novel, from its beginnings in the late seventeenth and early eighteenth centuries to its great popular flowering in the nineteenth, had been essentially what might be called a "public instrument," basing its view of what was significant in human affairs on a generally agreed standard. Its plot patterns were constructed out of incidents and situations which were seen to matter in human affairs equally by writer and reader. Changes in social or economic position or in marital situation were obvious and agreed indications of a significant alteration in a character's state, and such changes marked the crises of virtually all eighteenth- and nineteenth-century

plots. The author's attitude to his characters was essentially
one of observer; anything significant in his characters' behavior was at once indicated by a publicly observable movement toward some shift in status or fortune. The "two-travel-
ers-might-have-been-seen" opening was fairly common in the
nineteenth-century novel because it provided an appropriate
entry into a work of fiction in which the characters were de-
ployed before the reader (author and reader standing together, as it were, on the reviewing stand, with the author
where necessary whispering explanatory remarks into the
reader's ear) and revealed their inward development by their
outward behavior. The correlation between internal and external, between moral or intellectual development and appropriate observable action or inaction, was taken for granted.
And society was taken for granted. Men lived in a social and
economic world which was real, and the most real part of
their behavior was that which changed or in some way determined their position in that world.

All this is not surprising, for the English novel was after
all the characteristic product of the English middle classes,
and the middle classes have always been much concerned with
social and economic position, with the relation between public esteem and real worth. In Jane Austen (though her novels
appeared in the early nineteenth century) we find what is
really the fine flower of the eighteenth-century novel, the
projection of aspects of the human situation from a point of
view which takes a stratified society absolutely for granted and
which investigates the relation between private will and public status, between individual and social good, with extraordinary delicacy and wit. Every deviation from the implied
norm of reasonable adaptation of individuality to status and
of status to individuality yields its own brand of pride, preju-

dice, illusion, snobbery, selfishness, or folly, and life educates the educable in this adaptation: the success of the education is symbolized by a marriage in which personal desire, moral principle, and adequate fortune come together in each partner as well as in the couple. This is of course a wildly oversimplified description of Jane Austen's brilliant and subtle art; but the point relevant to the present investigation is that Jane Austen took a stable and hierarchic society absolutely for granted in the complete assurance that her readers shared the view of what is significant in human experience that is implied in the structure of her novels. As Virginia Woolf once remarked of Jane Austen, almost in envy: "To believe that your impressions hold good for others is to be released from the cramp and confinement of personality." One of the marks of the modern novelist is that he is unable to hold that belief.

Jane Austen was the last great English novelist to write before the Industrial Revolution changed the face of so much of England. After her, though the nineteenth-century novelist was equally committed to society and to a public sense of significance, it was to a society always changing and always challenging the perceptive observer to inquire somewhat uneasily into the real relationship between public esteem and true moral worth. The middle classes, who rose so spectacularly in wealth and power in the Victorian period, were (for reasons which need not here detain us) committed to respectability, to a surface show of conformity and decency, which lends itself easily to hypocrisy. Much Victorian fiction investigates the limits of hypocrisy, the ways in which and the degree to which vice can achieve the reputation of virtue by manifesting virtue's outward signs. It is true that the hypocrite had already a long history in English drama and fiction— Blifil in Fielding's *Tom Jones* is an example that springs at once to mind—but rather as a character-type to be satirized than as an inevitable product of the way society operates, which is the way the Victorian novelist tended to treat him. Yet the norms underlying Victorian plot-patterns remained public, and anything significant that occurred to a character was symbolized by change in fortune or status. Selection was still based on a criterion shared by reader and writer. It was clearly more significant for a character to run off with somebody else's wife than to drink a cup of tea or to suffer some inward shift in sensibility manifested by the merest flicker of an eyelid or perhaps by no outward sign at all. Human relationships were determined by human institutions, and the contact between people which those institutions made possible was real and satisfactory. In the modern novel, as we shall see, the novelist may have no assurance that it is the outward action which reveals the significant fact about his character, nor is he convinced that the public gestures provided by society—even by language, the most basic of all social instruments—can ever achieve real communication between individuals.

Every novelist must select from among the welter of events which make up human behavior: even if it were aesthetically desirable (which it obviously is not), it would clearly be physically impossible for a novelist to record *everything* which even his principal character was supposed to have done or thought or felt. If he selects, he selects on a principle. The older English novelist selected what were the significant things in the behavior of his characters on a principle publicly shared, and part of that publicly shared principle was the fact that what was significant in human events was itself manifested in publicly visible doing or suffering, in action or passion related to status or fortune.

The modern novelist is born when that publicly shared principle of selection and significance is no longer felt to exist, can no longer be depended on. The reasons for this breakdown of the public background of belief are related to new ideas in ethics, psychology, and many other matters as well as to social and economic factors. The relative stability of the Victorian world gave way to something much more confused and uncertain, and the shock to all established ideas provided by the First World War and the revelation of its horrors and futility helped to "carry alive into the heart by passion" (in Wordsworth's phrase) the sense of this breakdown. Of course, most ordinary people went on living their lives in accordance with the traditional morality and conventions of their fathers. It was only the sensitive *avant garde* who responded to this new feeling in the air and who believed, with Virginia Woolf, that they could no longer take it for granted that their impressions held good for others.

Some community of belief would seem to be necessary to all fictional art, and the apparent collapse of the public background represented a startling challenge to those novelists who were sensitive to it. They took up the challenge in various ways. Some, like Virginia Woolf, tried to make a personal sense of belief persuasive to the reader while he read by adopting some of the techniques of lyric poetry and building up a pattern of highly charged symbolic events and reveries told in a prose whose suggestive overtones and rhythmic compulsions worked on the experienced reader to reproduce in him the sense of significance out of which the author's vision arose. James Joyce, in his most characteristic work, sought for technical devices which would enable him to present all possible points of view simultaneously, showing the same persons and events as at once heroic and trivial, splendid and silly, important and unimportant. Joseph Conrad multiplied points of view in the telling of a story so that the tentativeness of all patterns of significance was established and the lonely truth at the heart of individual experience remained teasingly mysterious. D. H. Lawrence constructed his plots in such a way as to use social institutions as devices for probing the difficulties which lie in the way of proper human relationships and showed his characters discovering (or failing to discover) their own sense of meaning in those relationships through experiences that are essentially poetic and even mystical in nature and are projected by means of a quite new kind of fictional symbolism. The great surge of experimentation in fiction which went on in the 1920's and 1930's was in large measure caused by the novelists' search for devices that would enable them to solve the problem of the breakdown of a public sense of significance each in his own way. All the novelists mentioned brought some of the techniques of poetry into prose fiction. The novel inevitably became a subtler and in some senses a more difficult literary form than it had hitherto been—not necessarily better, because the great Victorian novelists at their best found perfect ways of dealing with their kind of fictional imagination, but more complex, because the modern novelist had additional problems to solve. The heroic age of experiment and expansion in the English novel was thus the product of what might be called a crisis in civilization, not the result of a wilful desire to "make it new" and be original for the sake of being original. Those novelists who were content with the old plot-patterns, who were content to emphasize the social documentary aspect of their art and to rely on the traditional changes in status and fortune to mark the high points of significance, often produced interesting and skilful novels, but novels which are now more documents of interest to the social historian or the historian of taste than illuminating explorations of aspects of the human situation. Virginia Woolf called Bennett, Wells, and Galsworthy "materialists" and complained that their work never really captured the inward vision. "Whether we call it life of spirit, truth or reality, this, the essential thing, has moved off, or on, and refuses to be contained any longer in such ill-fitting vestments as we provide."

Two other factors in addition to the breakdown of a public sense of significance help to produce what we have called the modern novel. One is the new concept of time as continuous flow rather than as a series of separate points, a concept independently enunciated in France, in Henri Bergson's concept of *la durée*, and in America by William James with his interest in the continuity of consciousness. Bergsonian ideas about time were in the air in the 1920's and influenced even those writers who had not read Bergson. It led to a suspicion of the old kind of plot which carried the characters forward from moment to moment in a precise chronological sequence, and there developed instead the kind of narrative texture that moved backward and forward with a new freedom to try to capture the sense of time as it actually operates in the human awareness of it. Closely linked to this new view of time was the new view of consciousness deriving in a general way from the work of Freud and Jung but concentrating on the fact of the multiplicity of consciousness, the presence in the given consciousness of all it had ever experienced and perhaps also of all that the race had experienced. The individual personality is the sum of the individual's memories, and to regard the past as something to be recalled by a conscious effort of memory is on this view to do violence to the facts of experience. The past exists always in the present, coloring and determining the nature of the present response, and to tell the truth about a character's reaction to any situation we must tell the whole truth about everything that has ever happened to him. The novelist who has been influenced by this view of time and consciousness will seek ways of communicating to the reader the simultaneity of different levels of consciousness and he will also realize that the whole truth about a mature person can be told by probing into his past through presenting the full texture of his present consciousness: this results in new kinds of fictional technique which are discussed in the next chapter.

Concern with individual consciousness, its multiplicity and ability to store up the whole of the individual's past history which is always relevant and always in operation in one way or another, leads to emphasis on the individual's loneliness. Every man is the prisoner of his own private consciousness, his unique train of association, which results in turn from his own unique past. The public gestures he makes toward communication can never be more than approximate, and he can never rely on their being understood. Indeed, insofar as the gestures are public they are bound to be falsified. The signals each individual flashes to the public world are bound to be in some degree misunderstood by that world, because every other person will read them in the light of that person's own private history. Society is thus in a sense unreal; its institutions inevitably blunt and coarsen the truth about the individual self, providing means of communication that can only distort. Loneliness is seen as the necessary condition of man. Yet the desire to communicate is also a deeply imbedded human instinct, and the desire to escape from loneliness one of the chief human preoccupations. To what extent is such an escape possible? The characters in Joyce's *Ulysses* who

are shown so often as drinking with and to each other in bars
—and communal drinking is one of the most primal gestures
of community, embodied in most religious rituals—making
contact with each other through social gestures of convivial-
ity, are at the same time shown as haunted by private thoughts
and emotions, the product of their individual past, which can
never be reflected in the social gesture. Social conventions
are seen as empty and mechanical, bearing no real relationship to the inner life of men. What E. M. Forster called "the
great society" is meaningless; at best only "the little society"
can have any validity. The carefully pursued friendship of
the small group may produce the only working society that
is possible. We can see the same theme pursued by American
novelists, notably by Ernest Hemingway, most of whose
novels are devoted to an exploration of the secret society, the
small community of men who by sharing experiences and
acting out a code together can impose some meaning on the
empty nothingness of social convention and pretension. In
Virginia Woolf's *Mrs. Dalloway* we see the heroine searching
for means of communicating with others: the novel is dominated by her intention of giving a party that evening, and it
is at the party that the climax occurs. Parties bring people
together; yet the unity they impose is superficial and in a
profound sense we are lonelier than ever in a crowd. While
Mrs. Dalloway seeks ways of establishing real contact with
others, she is at the same time dedicated to the preservation
of her own unique individuality, which is the basic condition
for an adequate existence. She had refused to accept Peter
Walsh, whom she loved, as a husband, because he had wanted
to dominate her personality, and had instead accepted a husband whose affection manifested itself more shyly and gave
her more freedom. Yet that freedom suggested loneliness

too, and she is haunted by images of herself in a lonely tower cut off from the cheerful conversation and activities of the people outside. Do we become part of all other people in death? she wonders at one point. At the same time the novel explores other aspects of loneliness and community, presenting in the madness and suicide of Septimus Warren Smith the dilemma of a man who, through his war experience, has lost all sense of the reality of the world of other people and who when forced to pretend that that reality is real for him by engaging in meaningless community gestures is driven to the final extremity.

In a different way, yet with a basic similarity of theme, Conrad explores again and again the ways in which social and political life are both necessary and corrupting. Lawrence sought a way out of this characteristic modern problem by insisting that true love consists not in merging (he castigated Whitman for believing in the merging of individuals) but in the recognition of the mystical core of otherness in the beloved, and, if that otherness is also a sexual otherness, the experience of being able to transcend the self through participation in otherness is more likely to be realized. Throughout all these novelists the question "How is love possible in a world of individuals imprisoned by their own private and unique consciousness?" is asked and probed in a great variety of ways. Loneliness is the great reality, love the great necessity: how can the two be brought together? The more public and social the world, the less real it is likely to be, so neither the earlier public view of significance nor the earlier confidence in the role of society can be maintained. Much modern fiction is the charting of a way out of solipsism.

Thus the three major factors that have influenced and in a sense produced the modern novel—the breakdown of public

agreement about what is significant in experience and therefore about what the novelist ought to select, the new view
of time, and the new view of the nature of consciousness—
co-operate to encourage the novelist to concentrate on aspects
of the human situation which were not the major concern of
earlier novelists (only one major earlier novelist, Laurence
Sterne, was concerned with loneliness and love in the modern
sense) and to discover new techniques for achieving their new
aims. There were of course other factors at work, but these
three seem to be those which most consistently, though in
very different ways, affected those great novelists of the first
half of this century who in their new insights and technical
experiments permanently enlarged the bounds of the art of
fiction.

2

Character

Should the personalities of characters in fiction emerge from a chronological account of a group of events and the characters' reactions to those events, or is it the duty of the novelist to take time off, as it were, in order to give a rounded description of the characters at the point when they are introduced into the story? Novelists have employed either of these two methods, and some have employed both at once. Sometimes the character as we see him first is a shadowy and indeterminate creature, but after his reactions to a chronological series of events have been presented we feel that he is now a living personality. In other novels we are given a descriptive portrait of the character first, so that we know what to expect, and the resulting actions and reactions of the character provide a filling-in and elaboration whose justness we can appreciate by comparison with the original portrait.

In Thomas Hardy's *Mayor of Casterbridge* there is no set description of Michael Henchard's character at the beginning of the book or, indeed, anywhere else. In the first chapter he is simply a young man, and Hardy continues to call him "the man" until the first episode is concluded. True, we have an account of Michael's physical appearance ("The man was of fine figure, swarthy, and stern in aspect," etc.) but that is all. There is no hint of his real nature—his personality. That

emerges as the story proceeds—emerges from the story itself, from the account of what Michael does, and the way in
which he reacts to the doings of others. It might be argued
that his character is not fully presented until the story is
concluded, and the only way Hardy has by then managed to
give us a full view of his character has been by taking him
through a long and varied sequence of events. Any criterion
of consistency we may apply can concern only the relation
of one action or reaction of Michael to another; there can be
no referring back to an original prose portrait, because the
author has not given us one.

That is one way of presenting character. The other, and
perhaps the commoner, way is illustrated as well as anywhere
in the third chapter of Trollope's *Barchester Towers*. The chapter is entitled "Dr. and Mrs. Proudie" and is a complete formal account of the characters of Dr. Proudie and his wife.
First a general sketch of Dr. Proudie's personality and
habits of mind, then an account of his career, then further
expansion of his present nature and attitude. Then Mrs.
Proudie is taken up and similarly treated. By the end of the
chapter we know exactly who and what these two characters
are: we know no more about their characters at the end of
the book—we have only seen the application to particular
events of the general principles already enunciated. The interest of the book lies in these events and in our noting and
approving how the characters run true to form throughout.

Most effective of all from the point of view of those whose
chief interest in fiction lies in its psychological aspects is the
technique which combines the foregoing two methods. Any
one of Jane Austen's novels would provide a good example of
this. *Emma*, for example, begins as follows:

> Emma Woodhouse, handsome, clever, and rich, with a comfortable home and happy disposition, seemed to unite some of the best blessings of existence; and had lived nearly twenty-one years in the world with very little to distress or vex her. . . .
>
> The real evils . . . of Emma's situation were the power of having rather too much her own way, and a disposition to think a little too well of herself; these were the disadvantages which threatened alloy to her many enjoyments. The danger, however, was at present so unperceived, that they did not by any means rank as misfortunes with her. . . .

And so on. In the first chapter we are given a fairly adequate sketch of Emma's character and circumstances. Yet we do not know Emma completely. A full understanding of her nature comes only after we have watched her reactions to the events which constitute the story and have studied her own part in the shaping of those events. Jane Austen has availed herself of both of our two methods: she starts with the inset character sketch, yet it is not complete, even as a character sketch, until we have seen Emma in her relations with Harriet Smith, Jane Fairfax, Mr. Elton, Mr. Knightley, and others. Whether or not there comes a point in the course of the novel, before the actual conclusion, where we feel that we know the real Emma, is a matter that individual readers may wrangle over; what concerns us here is to notice Jane Austen's method of showing us the kind of person that Emma is. Trollope shows us a known constant in varied circumstances, and our pleasure lies in recognizing the truth of the resulting description of behavior. Jane Austen shows us a partially known variant (variant for the reader just because partially known) in varied circumstances, and our pleasure lies in the progressively enhanced knowledge of that variant which the resulting description of behavior brings us—until there comes a point

at which the variant becomes a constant, as we know the limiting bounds within which it moves. Hardy shows us an unknown defining itself by its reactions to the circumstances
with which it is brought into contact. In all three cases a
consistent character portrait emerges, but in each case the
method of portraying—and the point at which the portrait is
complete—is different. It might be noted that in Jane Austen's
case minor characters are often portrayed by the first method:
Mr. Woodhouse, for example, is presented complete at his
first appearance and is made to act consistently throughout.

These two methods, separately or in combination, have
been the stock methods of presenting character in fiction
from the beginnings of the novel until modern times. Their
prototypes are, respectively, the "Character" as practiced
originally by Theophrastus and widely imitated in France
and England in the seventeenth century, and the simple adventure story. You put a character into a story, or you arrange a story so that a character emerges—to make a very
blunt distinction. In recent times, partly as a result of in-
creased speculation into the nature of states of consciousness,
writers have become dissatisfied with these traditional methods. They have realized that a psychologically accurate account of what a man is at any given moment can be given
neither in terms of a static description of his character nor in
terms of a group of chronologically arranged reactions to a
series of circumstances. They have become interested in those
aspects of consciousness which cannot be viewed as a pro-
gression of individual and self-existing moments, but which
are essentially dynamic rather than static in nature and are
independent of the given moment. The present moment is
specious; it denotes the ever fluid passing of the "already"
into the "not yet," and therefore retrospect and anticipation

constitute the very essence of consciousness at any specified time. In other words, the relation of consciousness to time is not the simple one of events to time, but is independent of chronological sequence in a way that events are not. Further, the quality of my experience of any new phenomenon (and hence my reaction to any new circumstance) is conditioned by a group of similar experiences scattered up and down through past time, the association of which with the present experience is what makes the present experience what it is. A novelist might try to indicate this by such digressions as, "That reminded him of . . . ," or "There flashed through his brain a memory of . . . ," or similar formulas, but modern writers have come to feel that this is too clumsy and artificial a way of expressing the mind's independence of chronological sequence. Some more fluid technique must be devised which will enable the author to utilize constantly those ever present contacts with the past which constitute the very stuff of consciousness. The static character sketch is, in the view of these writers, an arbitrary formalization of the real facts, while, on the other hand, to make the presentation of states of mind dependent on the step-by-step relation of a sequence of events in time is to impose on the mental activity of men a servile dependence on chronology which is not in accordance with psychological fact. It was as a way out of this difficulty (arising from a new realization of the complex and fluid nature of consciousness and the desire to utilize this realization in the portrayal of character) that the "stream of consciousness" technique was introduced into fiction.

Looked at from one point of view, the "stream of consciousness" technique is a means of escape from the tyranny of the time dimension. It is not only in distinct memories that the past impinges on the present, but also in much vaguer and more subtle ways, our mind floating off down some channel superficially irrelevant but really having a definite starting-off place from the initial situation; so that in presenting the characters' reactions to events, the author will show us states of mind being modified by associations and recollections deriving from the present situation (in a sense *creating* the present situation) but referring to a constantly shifting series of events in the past. Now, if this presentation of a state of mind is done with care and skill, the author will be able to kill two birds with one stone: he will be able to indicate the precise nature of the present experience of his character and at the same time he will be giving, incidentally, facts about the character's life previous to this moment—previous, in all probability, to the moment at which the book opens; and thus though the chronological scheme of the novel may comprise only a very limited time, one day for example, the characters will emerge complete, both historically and psychologically.

This technique is, as has been mentioned, an extension of the more traditional memory digression. But a story which claims to unite in mutual progress the event and the character's reaction to the event, so that the mental picture is always dependent on the physical situation, can exploit the points in consciousness where the past impinges on, and indeed conditions, the present only as a digression, as an exception to the rule, which will become wearisome and disintegrating to the story if indulged in to any extent. What the "stream of consciousness" technique enables the writer to do is to claim a validity for these references and impingements, a validity in their own right as it were, because it is through their means that the story is presented completely

and welded into a unity. The new method of describing states
of mind becomes a new technique of story-telling.

Consider the actual story in Virginia Woolf's *Mrs. Dalloway*. If we were to judge it by the chronological time scheme,
we should say that it was the story of one day in the life of a
middle-aged woman. But it is not that: the story embraces
much of Mrs. Dalloway's past life and her relations with
other characters in the past as well as in the present, so that,
even judging the story on the simple narrative level, we can
see that it is more than the story of one day's activity. This
inclusion of so much of Mrs. Dalloway's past life is made
possible by the way in which her ever changing state of mind
is described. True, the time sequence is marked off almost
rigidly by such an obvious device as the striking of clocks
(we shall discuss this point in more detail in a later chapter);
but the very reason why the chronological framework has to
be kept so constantly before the reader's attention is just because it is a framework, and nothing more. It is not the substance of the story, as it would be in any traditional novel; it
is the mere skeleton which supports the living flesh and blood
of the novel. Fixing her character physically at a given point
in time and space, Mrs. Woolf is free to follow the character's "stream of consciousness" up and down in these two dimensions. It is as though we are led away up a winding tributary, but, having previously marked with some easily distinguished object the point where the tributary joins the
main stream, we are able to find our way back at any moment. The significance of a novel like *Mrs. Dalloway* lies
—to continue the metaphor—in the tributaries explored
rather than in the main stream. The main stream is important only because it is from it that we take our bearings
and with reference to it that we chart our position at any

given moment. The line along which we move in the traditional chronological novel becomes, in a novel of this kind,
one of the axes of a graph on which the curve of our journey
is plotted, and we refer to the axis only when we want to
check up on our position.[1]

Thus the "stream of consciousness" technique is not
simply a method of describing states of mind, because the
method has implications for the whole technique of narrative
and character drawing. If we ask ourselves why Joyce in
Ulysses is able, while confining his chronological framework
to the events of a single day, to relate so much more than
merely the events of that single day and to make his hero
perhaps the most complete and rounded character in all fiction, the answer lies in the potentialities—potentialities for
narrative as well as for psychological analysis—of this new
method of describing mental attitudes.

But the advantages for psychological analysis need not be
minimized. The realization, which this technique implies, of
the fact that personality is in a constant state of unstable
equilibrium, that a mood is never anything static but a fluid
pattern "mixing memory with desire," marks an important
new development in the tradition of psychological fiction
that has come down to us from Richardson. Richardson tried
to present immediately the mood and thought of his characters by weaving his novels out of their letters. The defect
here, from the modern standpoint, is that letters written to a
given correspondent are bound to be subject to rigid formal
limitations which prohibit the direct and adequate expression
of states of mind. Only formalized aspects of an attitude can
be expressed to any given audience (as every audience, even
if the letter is a letter to the press, is a strictly defined and

[1] This point is discussed and elaborated in chap. x.

limited audience) however indefatigable a correspondent the
character may be. The inhibiting effect of the audience would
make the epistolary technique unacceptable to the modern
psychological novelist. The diary would seem a more helpful
device here than the letter; but the author will always be at a
loss to render convincing the desire of the character to express completely and effectively his states of mind with reference to the given circumstances. No, if the characters are
not to be either incredibly frank and self-conscious letter-
writers or continuously introverted egoists, the responsibility
for putting the "stream of consciousness" onto paper must
not be laid on the characters but assumed in full by the author. The technique of Dorothy Richardson or Virginia
Woolf or James Joyce is in this respect no more "real" than
any other: it is a convention like other conventions, and it
depends on our acceptance of the author's omniscience with
no limitation whatsoever; but, once the convention is accepted, it makes possible the presentation of aspects of personality and of states of mind which were not possible in fiction utilizing other techniques and other conventions.

That we are what we are in virtue of what we have been
is an obvious platitude; but the full utilization of the psychological aspects of this fact to build up a new technique in fiction is a comparatively recent development in the history of
literature. The wheel has come full circle since the days when
seventeenth-century wits wrote "characters" of types or ec-
centrics. Novelists who employ the "stream of consciousness" technique would deny that character *portrayal* is possible for the fiction writer at all: character is a process not a
state, and the truth about men's reactions to their environment—and what is a man's character but his reactions to environment, actual and potential?—can be presented only

through some attempt to show this process at work. An understanding of this view can help us to understand one of the main directive forces at work in modern fiction.

If we may return for a moment to the two traditional methods of presenting character discussed at the beginning of this chapter—the complete initial portrait followed by events which confirm the portrait and the emergence of the complete character from the action—we may note that a third method is frequently distinguished by students of fiction. This is the method which shows the character changing or developing, so that while the initial portrait is valid with reference to the situation presented at the beginning of the novel, it ceases to be valid by the time the novel is concluded. As a result of the circumstances in which the character finds himself throughout the course of the story, his nature is modified and we are finally confronted with a different person from the one we met at the beginning. Now, to distinguish this method as essentially a different technique seems to be the result of a certain confusion. It is of course possible to make a character really change in the course of the action: we know how in many popular novels the villain reforms at the end and becomes a good man. But such sudden and radical change as this—we recall Mr. Alfred Jingle's distressing conversion at the end of the *Pickwick Papers*—is never convincing in terms of psychological probability. Development, however, as distinct from such crude change, is more regular in good fiction. This is in essence but one aspect of our second method, when the character, incompletely presented at the beginning, does not emerge completely until the action has taken place. The final character is different, in the sense that events have made actual elements in his nature which before were only potential. The completeness of a character is judged by the degree to which its potentialities are realized. Thus, one reason why there is no complete portrayal at the beginning, why the portrayal is not complete until after we have seen the character in action, may be because the character was not meant to be a complete character until after these events had brought to light what was hitherto dormant. There is such a thing as an incomplete character in life. It may be such a character that the author introduces to us at the beginning of his story, while eventually we see the character made complete by experience. It will be seen that this is a modification of what we have called the second method rather than a quite separate method.

This point may be made clearer if we take an example from drama, where this development is more regular. Take the stock example of *King Lear*. King Lear is a different man at the end of the play from the man he was in Act I. Experience has altered his attitude, and we can actually see that process of modification at work throughout the play. Yet the circumstances presented in the play do not so much *change* Lear's character as bring out aspects of it which hitherto events had not conspired to release. This is a very different thing from the formal conversion of a villain to a reformed character. A character is not fully revealed until brought into the necessary testing circumstances, and an author can introduce us to a character either before or after he has met with such circumstances. There is a difference between change as the fulfilment of latent potentialities and change as the entire alteration of what previously existed. Consider Jane Austen's *Emma* again. True, Emma's character develops: she is more sensible in her attitude to specific things when we leave her than she was when we found her. But this is simply because her inherent common sense, a characteristic of hers all along, has had an opportunity of confronting experiences with which she was hitherto unfamiliar. Her rationality has applied itself to new premises and made the necessary deductions; and in the future she will always be in possession of those deductions. The change in Emma is of course very trivial when compared with that in Lear; but the difference is one of degree and not of kind. (Changes which are a result of physical or biological development are naturally in quite a different category. An adult is a different character from the child he once was. It might even be argued that for the purposes of plot in fiction they represent two separate characters. Novels whose central figure is shown progressing from infancy to manhood are liable to be episodic; no single presentation of character emerges from the work as a whole.)

What has the "stream of consciousness" technique to offer in presenting development in character? The situation here is very different from that present with either of the traditional methods; because by the adequate exploitation of states of mind and by following up all the paths suggested by the impinging of the past, in its multifarious variety, on the present, the nature of potentiality in character can be indicated even without our being shown the occurrence of events that would make those potentialities actual. The most interesting case in point here is the character of Stephen Dedalus in *Ulysses*. We see Stephen still a young man immature, foolish, in many respects undeveloped. We are not shown him at all in his maturity—nothing in the book anticipates that day in June, 1904. Yet the fulness of implication provided by Joyce's method of presenting the consciousness of his characters is such that by the time the book closes we know the whole of Stephen, even though the whole of him is not yet, as it were, made actual. We can see the germ of the future

in the present and without looking beyond the present. In
Mrs. Dalloway, too, though the method is applied to her
very much less intensely (and she is already a woman near
the end of her life), we have a feeling by the end of the book
that we know not only what she is and has been but what she
might have been—we know all the unfulfilled possibilities in
her character. In a character whose life is almost complete,
unfulfilled possibilities are mere "might have beens"; in a
character who has not yet reached complete maturity, such
potentialities reveal also what may be.

If Joyce's method had been applied to the character of
Lear it would have been possible, within a chronological
framework comprising one day in Lear's life before the
tragedy occurred, to make the reader aware of those potentialities in his character that in the play we do not see until
they are made actual by events. The "stream of consciousness" method, at its most subtle and most intense, is able to
achieve by depth what the traditional method achieves by
extension. It provides a method of presenting character outside time and place; in the double sense that, first, it separates
the presentation of consciousness from the chronological sequence of events, and, second, it enables the quality of a given
state of mind to be investigated so completely, by means of
pursuing to their end the remote mental associations and suggestions, that we do not need to wait for time to make the potential actual before we can see the whole.

3

Joseph Conrad

The nineteenth-century novel was anchored in a world of public value agreed on by reader and writer, and its plot-pattern was determined by changes in fortune and status on the part of the principal characters. Such changes combined public and private significance. This does not mean that nineteenth-century novelists equated social esteem with individual moral worth: on the contrary, the commonest theme of the Victorian novel is the disparity between gentility and morality, between the claims of society and the claims of genuine personal integrity: this is the theme of Dickens' *Great Expectations* as it is of Thackeray's *Vanity Fair*. But, however much the Victorian novelist may criticize the society of his time, his war with society is never radical enough to sweep away public criteria of what is significant in human action. George Eliot's *Middlemarch* presents a complexly critical picture of Victorian provincial society at work, and this picture both provides the context for and is reinforced by the individual moral and psychological problems with which her characters are involved; but the pattern is woven throughout from public symbols—marriage, gain or loss of money, gain or loss of public reputation. Public reaction to individual behavior might be wrong, but it is not wrongly directed—i.e., it is concerned with the things that it ought to be concerned about even where it takes a position shown by the author to be an improper one. Even Hardy, a novelist devastatingly critical of the assumptions of his age, carries his plots forward by public symbols, and it is worth considering the parts played in *The Mayor of Casterbridge*, *Tess of the D'Urbervilles*, and *Jude the Obscure* by marrying and giving in marriage, gain or loss of fortune, failure or success in social ambition. The modern novelist (in the sense in which the term is being used in this book) is born when such public machinery is no longer used in order to achieve the plot-pattern, and the true inwardness of a character's moral and psychological problems can be revealed only by removing him from the distorting mirror of a public sense of significance and exploring the truth about him in an isolation either real or symbolic. Are human relations really possible, or is every individual condemned ultimately to remain in the prison of his own incorrigibly private consciousness? The "great society" is not a real society but only a mechanical ritual of empty gesturing; at most, only the "little society" can produce and reflect value, the communion of friends acting out a ritual that will shore them against the ruins of a world whose slogans have become merely verbal, the discovery through sex of the otherness of the beloved and the realization that in the awareness of true otherness rather than in merging lies true love, even the dissolution of personality through the willed immersion in the flux of time or the deliberate identification of the subjective vision with the whole of reality—characteristic responses of, respectively, Hemingway, Lawrence, and Virginia Woolf.

It is in this sense that Joseph Conrad is the first important modern novelist in English: his finest novels and stories are all concerned, directly or obliquely, with situations to which public codes—*any* public codes—are inapplicable, situations which yield a dark and disturbing insight which cannot be related to any of the beliefs or rules which make human societies possible. How far Conrad's personal history as a Pole who left his native country as a youngster to become a merchant seaman and became British in nationality and language only in adult life helps to explain the deep skepticism about the possibility of true public value that is found in so much of his work is no part of the present study to investigate; but the fact remains that when his genius is working most powerfully the world of significance which he creates is at furthest remove from the world of public significance created by the great Victorian and eighteenth-century novelists. Conrad himself sometimes talked as though life on board a merchant vessel represented a microcosm of human society which effectively tested such ethical norms as fidelity and showed their central place in all human affairs; but Conrad's interpretations of his own work—especially those he wrote late in life—are notoriously oversimplified and even falsified. *The Nigger of the Narcissus*, his first really important novel, published in 1897, is far from an exhibition of the moral effectiveness of the sailor's code even though there are moments when simple courage and steadfastness *do* win through and save the ship. The dying Negro seaman, James Wait, puts a curse on the ship by arousing in the crew feelings of humanity which are nevertheless at bottom feelings of self-interest. "The latent egoism of tenderness to suffering appeared in the developing anxiety not to see him die." Even the apparently outward-going affections are a form of selfishness and can provide no escape from the prison of the self: the only adequate escape is the escape into the total self-forgetfulness of arduous physical duty performed under the compulsion of the sea and its dangers, but though this yields survival it cannot go further and suggest what the survivors are to do with their lives.

James Wait's presence on the ship tests the reality of the ship's company as a microcosm of a valid society; he "humanises" them and in the process corrupts them. "He was demoralising. Through him we were becoming highly humanised, tender, complex, excessively decadent: we understood the subtlety of his fear, sympathised with all his repulsions, shrinkings, evasions, delusions—as though we had been over-civilised and rotten, and without any knowledge of the meaning of life." Such a passage suggests that far from being a microcosm of society a ship's company is an escape from the problems of social relations and human sympathy posed by society, and if any such problems are raised on board ship the result is demoralizing. This is not, of course, Conrad's consistent position—elsewhere he uses life at sea as a means of probing certain kinds of moral value and social responsibility—but in this novel he deliberately makes sympathy, a necessary social virtue, into a corrupting form of self-identification which has no place in the outward-going virtues of good seamanship. The curious relationship between the dishonest malingerer Donkin (the least seaman-like of all on board) and James Wait further associates sympathy with evil. Only the old sailor Singleton among the men is indifferent to Wait and his illness, and Singleton is only acceptable in the impersonal world of necessary duty: we see him after the ship has been righted from its long lurch to leeward as a lonely symbolic figure of selfless action posed in an almost Christlike attitude:

Apart, far aft, and alone by the helm, old Singleton had deliberately tucked his white beard under the top button of his glistening coat. Swaying upon the din and tumult of the seas, with the whole battered length of the ship launched forward in a rolling rush before his steady old eyes, he stood rigidly still, forgotten by all, and with an attentive face. In front of his erect figure only the two arms moved crosswise with a swift and sudden readiness, to check or urge again the rapid stir of circling spokes. He steered with care.

But when the ship has reached port and Singleton disembarks to become a member of ordinary society he is seen as simply a dirty old man:

> Singleton came up, venerable—and uncertain as to daylight; brown drops of tobacco juice hung in his white beard; his hands, that never hesitated in the great light of the open sea, could hardly find the small pile of gold in the profound darkness of the shore. "Can't write?" said the clerk, shocked. "Make a mark, then." Singleton painfully sketched in a heavy cross, blotted the page. "What a disgusting old brute," muttered the clerk.

James Wait and Donkin alone on the "Narcissus" appealed to what might be called land values, invoking the social world of rights as well as duties, of compassion and self-pity as well as command and obedience, and in doing so they spread corruption; for a crew at sea is *not* a microcosm of normal human society. Or should we say rather that a crew at sea *is* a microcosm of human society but reveals that society as such is inevitably corrupt, that the ties of affection and hatred that link men in community are really disguises for emotional self-indulgence and self-love, that human relationships are never what they seem to be, that (to put it bluntly) love is an illusion? In Conrad's best novels no patterns of love and communion ever really work, society is not really nourished by human contacts and sympathies: love and loyalty are corrupted in *Nostromo* by the silver of the mine and the "material interests" it represents, but Conrad makes it perfectly clear that any alternative kind of society to that produced by the "material interests" is even more corrupting. When Conrad faced the implications of his own most inspired writing, he was afraid of what he saw, and retreated into a more conventional position to produce stories in which the moral pattern was nicely divided into black and white. At the end of *Victory*, Heyst, the solitary man who has professed to scorn the world, learns too late his mistake and exclaims "Woe to the man whose heart has not learned while young to hope, to love—and to put its trust in life!" It is a melodramatic and unconvincing exclamation, just as the whole ending of *Victory* is melodramatic and unconvincing, and it shows Conrad shying away (as he did so often in later life) from the implications of his own vision. That that vision was a profoundly pessimistic one no careful reader of his work will deny. One aspect of his pessimism is the recurring implication that man's fate is inevitably to be solitary and any attempt to break out of the prison of the self into real communion with others is doomed to failure or dishonesty or corruption or unreality. A curious corollary of this is that the only true communion one can achieve is the unwilled and startling communion with those whom we would like to think our opposites, as when Marlow achieves his shattering communion with Kurtz in "Heart of Darkness" or the Captain in "The Secret Sharer" realizes his strange identity with the murderer whom he has sheltered. To grow up, to become mature, is for Conrad to come to terms with such identities. Lord Jim is destroyed because, perpetually immature, he refuses to recognize the kinship claimed by Gentleman Brown, the kinship with evil; but the kinship, however superficially remote, is really there, and to fight it is to invite self-destruction. Youth can and should be immature, can and should have illusions, can and should see disaster as adventure and mishap as opportunity; that is the whole point of Conrad's story "Youth," which is an impressive evocation of this state of mind in a most persuasively realized context. There is something engaging and even admirable about the illusions of youth; but they become dangerous if they persist after experience, when they foster self-delusion and that special kind of romanticism that Conrad probes so cunningly in *Lord Jim*.

Lord Jim (1900) has certain weaknesses resulting largely from the fact that it was originally conceived as a short story (dealing only with the "Patna" incident) and was later elaborated, with the well-known shifts in point of view and manipulations of time-sequence, into a complex exploration —of problems of guilt, pride, self-deception, and related moral ambiguities—that reveals much that is central in Conrad's attitude and technique. Marlow, who tells much of Jim's story, reveals by his hesitations and questionings his own uncertainty about the meaning of it all. The central situation is itself ambiguous. Jim, the imaginative and accomplished young first mate of the "Patna" who allowed himself to be persuaded by the skipper and others to leave what he considered the doomed ship with the crew and passengers sleeping on board and has his mate's certificate revoked by the court of inquiry in consequence, is the only one of the three guilty men who remains to face the music, to attend the inquiry, to hear his sentence. He is better than the other two; if, under circumstances that he cannot properly explain even to himself, he allowed himself to jump from the doomed ship, he nevertheless is convinced that there were some special, strange, indefinable extenuating circumstances which miti-

gate his guilt and account for everything. This is a kind of
self-deception, clearly. But is his remaining to face the inquiry a sign of grace or a sign of false romanticism? Is he as
different from the other two guilty men as he imagines? Is
he really running away when he thinks he is facing it out?
He gets a job as a water clerk, but as soon as somebody arrives in the port who knows about the "Patna" Jim throws
up his job and moves further eastward, and so he moves further and further away from the outposts of Western civilization until he reaches his final haven and his final test in Patusan: is this courage or cowardice—or a bewildering mixture
of both? Jim will not face the truth about himself; he insists
on regarding his past as a cruel accident. He wants to undo
it by some heroic gesture, some ideal achievement. The position he makes for himself in Patusan, as savior and protector
of a native community, is in some respects an ideal achievement, yet it is at the same time an escape and an excuse. He
betrays his people—unintentionally—to Gentleman Brown
because he accepts the blackmail of identification between
Brown and himself, insinuated by Brown, and then makes
amends to *himself* by going to his certain and useless death
in a gesture of purely romantic histrionics. Is this his ultimate
vindication or his ultimate failure? He goes to his death
against the entreaties of the devoted Jewel, replying to her
protests with the announcement that "Nothing can touch me"
—said "in a last flicker of superb egotism."

Whose diagnosis is the right one? Marlow himself cannot
be sure. The French naval lieutenant is unable to give an
opinion on what life may be worth when honor is gone. The
benevolent and wise Mr. Stein, who is the means of giving
Jim the opportunity to redeem himself in Patusan—if it is
really a redemption—explains that Jim "is romantic—ro-

mantic. . . . And that is very bad." He has his own prescription. "A man that is born falls into a dream like a man who falls into the sea. If he tries to climb out into the air as inexperienced people endeavour to do, he drowns. . . . The way is to the destructive element submit yourself, and with the exertions of your hands and feet in the water make the deep, deep sea keep you up. . . . In the destructive element immerse." But Stein himself is a romantic German, and the conversation with Marlow in which he gives this prescription in the dusk of an eastern night is curiously self-indulgent. In any case, his advice is ambiguous. Does it mean that a man must not try to escape from his dream into the world of reality for that will kill him? If it means this, is he not preaching living in an unreal world? In a sense, was not that what Jim had been doing in refusing to admit that he had failed the test and seeking always for an explanation and a way of vindication? Stein and his destructive element are themselves parts of the puzzle, not Conrad's solution.

Lord Jim is not a study of a romantic young man redeeming a terrible moment of cowardice by later bravery and self-sacrifice, nor is it a study of a weak young man whose vanity makes him unable to come to terms with his weakness. Yet each of these descriptions is in some sense and in some degree true. Jim's final act of surrendering his life is heroic, though it is also exhibitionist and useless. And in a sense his failure on the "Patna" was not a straightforward act of betrayal or cowardice. The cause was partly his too lively imagination —and imagination, we must remember, is the sympathetic faculty which destroyed the morale of the crew of the "Narcissus." Jim visualized with great clarity what would happen if the packed body of sleeping pilgrims were to be awakened to a sense of their inevitable doom (as Jim considered it); he saw in his own lively mind the panic and horror; and as a result he allowed himself to believe that it would be best for all concerned if they sank quietly and asleep with the ship. But the ship didn't sink, and Jim's decision became in cold, objective fact, a gross dereliction of duty. Jim will never admit that it was a decision; it was something that happened to him. When explaining the events of that night to Marlow, he tells of how the others had got into the boat and then eventually "I had jumped. . . . It seems." He insists to Marlow that he was prepared "for all the difficulties that can beset one on land and water." "He had been rehearsing dangers and defences, expecting the worst, rehearsing his best." What actually happened fitted in to none of his rehearsals. When Marlow remarks, "It is always the unexpected that happens," Jim brushes the remark aside. Yet he might have known. We are shown a preview of the "Patna" disaster in the opening chapter, when Jim delays in joining the rescue party from the training-ship and finds suddenly that he is too late, has lost his opportunity. We are told also in chapter ii that Jim became chief mate "when yet very young, . . . without ever having been tested by those events of the sea that show in the light of day the inner worth of a man, the edge of his temper, and the fibre of his stuff; that reveal the quality of his resistance and the secret truth of his pretences, not only to others but also to himself." Jim never learned "the secret truth of his pretences." Were his pretenses vindicated in the end? The answer remains ambiguous. But one of his moral deficiencies was that he was unable to cope with the secret sharer.

There is another character in *Lord Jim* who cannot cope with the secret sharer: that is Captain Brierly, one of the assessors at the inquiry. Enormously successful in his maritime career, envied by all, Brierly yet has a secret sense of guilt which is revealed to him as he listens to the facts of Jim's case. Less than a week after the inquiry he commits suicide by jumping over the side of his ship. The incident is not fully realized in the story and it is left deliberately mysterious. But Conrad leaves us in no doubt that Brierly sees himself in Jim, for reasons and in a manner unrevealed to us, and the recognition compels his suicide. "Who can tell what flattering view he had induced himself to take of his own suicide?" asks Marlow, and the question could even more appropriately be asked of Jim, whose final death is really a form of suicide.

The Patusan scenes in *Lord Jim* are the least satisfactory, and Jim's establishment of himself as the father of a Malay community is altogether too facilely presented. Yet the novel survives it. The questionings and ambiguities of Marlow's narrative and the shifts of focus provided by Conrad in the unfolding of the story succeed in giving it the dimensions he requires for it. If you cannot be simple-minded and unimaginative like Captain MacWhirr of *Typhoon*, you are likely to find your good qualities warring against each other. Sensitivity, imagination, sympathy—they all can corrupt, either by encouraging self-deception or in other ways. And pride, which is necessary if a man is to have confidence in himself and his code (it is significant that the evil skipper of the "Patna" has no pride at all), can also produce self-flattering illusions and escapist exhibitionism. The code we live by may be all right for the ordinary man or the ordinary moment, but if when the testing point comes either the man has too much imagination or the moment is of a wholly unanticipated kind, the code is challenged with disturbing results. To face the wholly unanticipated successfully requires either stolidness or high qualities that transcend imagination and sympathy. Jim falls between the alternatives. He is not wholly guilty, we cannot help feeling, for the effect of that "I had jumped. . . . It seems" is to make the reader share Jim's sense of disbelief in his own guilt. Yet the reader is aware at the same time that he ought not to share this disbelief. The measure of the success of this unequal novel lies in the degree to which Conrad's method of narration has involved the reader in this way.

In many of his novels and stories Conrad draws on his own experiences at sea or elsewhere, but there is no correlation between the degree of autobiography and the merit of the work. The late novel, *The Arrow of Gold* (1919), draws considerably on autobiography, but autobiography deliberately surrounded by a fog of heavily romantic atmosphere so that character and action fade into mood; the mood has its own rather vague appeal, but in the last analysis the novel is simply an invitation to the reader to surrender to atmosphere and to adolescent musing. Autobiography cannot be successfully distanced by vagueness, but it *can* be successfully distanced by the introduction of an intermediary character such as Marlow whose response to the situation he is describing is sufficiently tentative, even at times bewildered, to suggest to the reader its complexity and moral ambiguity. Thus "Heart of Darkness" (published in *Youth and Other Stories* in 1902) draws largely on Conrad's own experiences on the Congo River, but it is told in the first person by Marlow, who is looking back on this first truly adult of his experiences of whose meaning he is still not wholly clear, but whose intensity and disturbing quality remain vividly with him. The experience was in fact his introduction to the adult world; it marked the end of his youth and also it brought with it an uneasy knowledge of the inadequacy of all public formulations of human standards and human motives, so that on his return from the Congo he feels cut off from ordinary people and their ordinary activities and attitudes:

> I found myself back in the sepulchral city resenting the sight of people hurrying through the streets to filch a little money from each other, to devour their infamous cookery, to gulp their unwholesome beer, to dream their insignificant and silly dreams. They trespassed upon my thoughts. They were intruders whose knowledge of life was to me an irritating pretense, because I felt so sure they could not possibly know the things I knew. Their bearing, which was simply the bearing of commonplace individuals going about their business in the assurance of perfect safety, was offensive to me like the outrageous flauntings of folly in the face of a danger it is unable to comprehend. I had no particular desire to enlighten them, but I had some difficulty in restraining myself from laughing in their faces so full of stupid importance.

Conrad in "Heart of Darkness" records with ironic precision his awareness of the realities of colonialism in Africa, of the greed and selfishness which lay behind the idealistic professions of the trading companies, but the story is not at all an anti-imperialist fable, for the truth about both white man and black man in Europe and in Africa will not respond to simple moral formulation. Conrad was a conservative who had no illusions about politics and full awareness of the mockeries and hypocrisies which underlie the arguments and attitudes of supporters of things as they are; he is a conservative because he cannot conceive of any revolutionary activity being either honest or effective; and this combination of conservatism and lack of illusions (or perhaps his lack of illusions amounted itself to an illusion?) necessarily implied a deep pessimism about the possibilities of political and

social action, a pessimism which is most fully worked out in
Nostromo, where among other things we see, in the character
and fate of Charles Gould, idealist motives and material interests becoming so inextricably involved that the latter destroy the former without any conscious change of motive or
moral position on the part of the man who is caught up in this
destruction. In the end every individual of stature is either
driven back into isolation or forced by some unexpected and
shattering experience to recognize some sort of identity with
his own opposite, as Marlow recognizes some sort of identity
with Kurtz.

What is the relation between motive and actuality? Can
an "idea" justify robbery and exploitation? "They grabbed
what they could get for the sake of what was to be got. It
was just robbery with violence, aggravated murder on a
great scale, and men going at it blind—as is very proper for
those who tackle a darkness. The conquest of the earth,
which mostly means the taking it away from those who have
a different complexion or slightly flatter noses than ourselves,
it not a pretty thing when you look into it too much. What
redeems it is the idea only." This is Marlow talking, and
Conrad does not make wholly clear how ironical (if at all)
that last sentence is. Shortly afterwards, describing how he
looked at a map of Africa and observed the amount of red
marking British Colonial territory, Marlow observes:
"There was a vast amount of red—good to see at any time,
because one knows that some real work is done in there. . . ."
But what becomes of the notion of "some real work" in the
light of the story as a whole? The whole tenor of "Heart of
Darkness" is to cast doubt on this kind of moral category.
Marlow is softened up, as it were, for his final vision of evil
and his odd sense of identity with it by his progress first

along the African coast and then up the river. His first vision of natives is one of energy and vitality, yet oddly disturbing as well as comforting. And his first sight of white "progress" is a French man-of-war shelling the bush, an action of sheer insanity:

Now and then a boat from the shore gave one a momentary contact with reality. It was paddled by black fellows. You could see from afar the white of their eyeballs glistening. They shouted, sang; their bodies streamed with perspiration; they had faces like grotesque masks—these chaps; but they had bone, muscle, a wild vitality, an intense energy of move-ment, that was as natural and true as the surf along their coast. They wanted no excuse for being there. They were a great comfort to look at. For a time I would feel I belonged still to a world of straightforward facts; but the feeling would not last long. Something would turn up to scare it away. Once, I remember, we came upon a man-of-war anchored off the coast. There wasn't even a shed there, and she was shell-ing the bush. It appears the French had one of their wars going on thereabouts. . . . In the empty immensity of earth, sky, and water, there she was, incomprehensible, firing into a continent. Pop, would go one of the six-inch guns; a small flame would dart and vanish, a little white smoke would dis-appear, a tiny projectile would give a feeble screech—and nothing happened. Nothing could happen. There was a touch of insanity in the proceeding, a sense of lugubrious drollery in in the sight; and it was not dissipated by somebody on board assuring me earnestly that there was a camp of natives—he called them enemies!—hidden out of sight somewhere.

The sense of utter irrationality, of some horrible meaning-lessness, increases as Marlow proceeds up the river, to hear more and more about the successful yet frightful Kurtz, whom he finally meets, dying, surrounded by evidence of his surrender to the atavistic temptations of a corrupted primitive civilization. Kurtz had been the apostle of progress who had been destroyed by his own imagination and vitality to become at the same time the fanatical enemy and the obsessed slave of the savage culture he had wished to redeem and westernize. His idealistic report to the International Society for the Suppression of Savage Customs—"a beautiful piece of writing"—begins with soaring optimistic eloquence in discussing the good the white man can do among these primitive people; but "at the end of that moving appeal to every altruistic sentiment it blazed at you, luminous and terrifying, like a flash of lightning in a serene sky: 'Exterminate all the brutes!' " The nature of Kurtz's greatness and of his influence is never directly described, but only hinted at obliquely through a number of incidents and references, but that in his way he *was* great is made clear enough. He achieved in the end "his own exalted and terrible degradation" through having seen through everything and come to believe in absolutely nothing. "I had to deal with a being to whom I could not appeal in the name of anything high or low." Yet as he lies dying "the shade of the original Kurtz" sometimes spoke in words of idealism or of fierce egotism (the two are now seen as related if not identified) before his last words express his final insight: "The horror! The horror!" If this is somewhat overmelodramatic, and if Marlow in his description of his voyage and the atmosphere of the places and people he visited tends to fall back on strings of heavily suggestive adjectives which tell us nothing very precisely, this is because Marlow is shown as himself not fully understanding the meaning of his experience. Yet the author knows what he is doing. He has not invented Marlow as an excuse for his own ignorance of the meaning of a part of his autobiography. The fact that Marlow is unable to formulate the meaning of Kurtz's metamorphosis and death and of his own response to the heart of darkness means that they do not respond to any formulation possible to a man of action such as a ship's captain.

One reason for the impossibility of formulation is the wide applicability of the experience. For Conrad makes it quite clear that the heart of darkness is a symbolic experience of what lies at the heart of much human profession and activity. Commerce, progress, imperialism, politics, society—in the last analysis they are based on what does not bear looking into. And in the last analysis they are not *real*, but conscious or unconscious covers for something else—perhaps merely for a great nothingness. Again we have the suggestion that outside individual experience there is perhaps no reality, that society can never be wholly real. London is involved in the heart of darkness as much as Africa. The story is told on board a cruising yawl on the Thames near Gravesend while Marlow and his friends are waiting for the ebb tide. Marlow begins by thinking of the Romans first coming to what was for them a heart of darkness on the Thames and at the end he looks out on the darkening sky and water and sees the river as leading away to some black unknown: "The offing was barred by a black bank of cloud and the tranquil water-way leading to the uttermost ends of the earth flowed sombre under an overcast sky—seemed to lead into the heart of an immense darkness." Normal life can only go on if we ignore that darkness. When Marlow returns to Belgium to bring the news of Kurtz's death to his "intended," he finds himself unable to tell her the truth about the circumstances in which he died, but fulfils her hope and expectation by telling her that he died with her name on his lips. She says that she "wants something to live with," and she is given a lie, which makes life possible for her. The question of the morality of

Marlow's conduct does not arise. The point is that the conventions of civilized life cannot bear too much reality.

In *Nostromo* (1904), his most sustained and complex novel,
Conrad pursues a similar theme using a much wider canvas
and with a much more deliberate use of historical and political as well as psychological material. The setting of the story
in the imaginary South American republic of Costaguana is
a remarkable tour de force; Costaguana is almost painfully
real in every aspect of its history and geography and its
reality is conveyed to the reader not only by the persuasive
use of detail but even more by the uncanny perceptiveness
with which Conrad traces the impact on the behavior and
attitude of his characters of the political and economic forces
inevitably set in motion when a backward state suddenly
finds itself possessed of independence and in the orbit of the
Western industrial world. The various revolutions which
form the history of Costaguana are not employed by Conrad
simply as devices for projecting crises which move the action
along in the desired direction; they are shown—with an
accuracy that any historian of nationalism, imperialism, capitalism, and democracy in the nineteenth and twentieth centuries well might envy—as part of the pattern which is bound
to develop, and has in fact so often developed, under the
given historical and geographical circumstances. Mr. Irving
Howe has commented on the startling resemblance between
the imaginary political history of Costaguana as Conrad told
it in 1904 and the actual political history of Cuba from 1933
on. But this insight into forces at work in the modern world
is used only to provide the background of the novel, to ground
it in an over-all reality that the reader has no choice but to
know and accept. There is more than the willing suspension
of disbelief here: the story sounds as though it could not pos-

sibly have been invented, so that in answer to such a question as "Why did Conrad make the old inn-keeper Giorgio Viola an Italian and a Garibaldino?" we are at first tempted to say in surprise "Why, because obviously Viola *was* an Italian and a Garibaldino." The impact of the story is so utterly persuasive. Only later, on reflecting on the whole complex pattern of the novel, we realize that Viola, who really stands outside the action almost as a sad chorus, represents an older and simpler kind of national revolutionary democratic faith, of the kind that inspired Garibaldi and his followers but which in the modern world no longer corresponds to anything that goes on or could go on. For *Nostromo* is a novel about the springs of political action in the modern world, or at least in certain parts of the modern world, and, as we might by now expect of Conrad, the view that comes across is that political action can never be real and at the same time it can never be avoided. When we say it can never be real, that does not mean that it cannot alter the lives of men; it does, sometimes with appalling cruelty; but it is never directly related to what it professes to be concerned with and never deals with (still less solves) the problems it is commonly supposed to deal with.

From one point of view, *Nostromo* can be seen as the pitiless exposure of how "material interests" (a phrase that recurs again and again in the book) can corrupt both a society and individuals, with a positively Marxist emphasis on economic predestination. Yet this is to misread the novel. It is true that the silver mine of Sulaco so obsesses Charles Gould that it divides him from his wife and claims him utterly; it is true also that it is silver which corrupts the faithful Nostromo and silver which motivates the actions both of local adventurers and foreign speculators. Material interests and the politics they demand do indeed corrupt. But they also *reveal*. *Nostromo* is very far from presenting a picture of a good or even a potentially good society being corrupted by the pressures of modern capitalism, even though those pressures are exhibited with extraordinary clarity and persuasiveness. The Ribiera government, which is the one supported by foreign investors and which stands for material interests, is seen in the end to mean oppression and injustice. Dr. Monygham, whose sardonic and self-distrustful voice is almost always the voice of truth in this novel, answers Mrs. Gould's question about the future, a question she asks toward the conclusion of the novel, with a bitter outburst: "There is no peace and no rest in the development of material interests. They have their law, and their justice. But it is founded on expediency, and is inhuman; it is without rectitude, without the continuity and the force that can be found only in a moral principle. . . ." And Mrs. Gould's final vision of the mine to which her husband had devoted so much passionate work and thought is a vision of a terrible destructive force, "possessing, consuming, burning up the life of the Costaguana Goulds; . . ." She sees herself "surviving alone the degradation of her young ideal of life, of love, of work—all alone in the Treasure House of the World." Yet Conrad offers no alternative that is better—none indeed that is nearly as good. This is a point to be emphasized. *Nostromo* may be a political novel but it is not an ideological novel nor is it a novel of political protest or propaganda. The regime of Guzman Bento, against which the Ribierist movement had revolted, is shown as a government of fiendish cruelty and preposterously naïve corruption, while the various elements which in turn revolt against the Ribiera government are portrayed with bitter mockery as motivated purely by a clownish selfishness and capable of the most irrational atrocities. Capitalist democracy dependent on foreign investment (which from one point of view is also foreign exploitation) is shown as the inevitable conclusion of Costaguana's series of revolutions, and the solution toward which the old-fashioned aristocratic liberalism of Don José Avellanos is bound to lead, even though Don José himself does not realize this any more than he understands any of the realities of the modern world. So if the novel ends with a picture of the silver mine, symbol of modern capitalism and of material interests as well as of economic imperialism, crushing out the reality of human relationships from daily human life, this is not presented so as to suggest that any other possible solution would be more hopeful. It is the despairing politics of the pessimistic conservative. Society cannot work morally.

Yet man needs society: if society cannot work, neither can loneliness. Martin Decoud, the sophisticated Parisian journalist who becomes involved in Costaguana politics because of his love for Don José's daughter, makes his cynical comments on the ambitions and professions of Costaguana politicians of both sides, speaking with an uncommitted voice, emphasizing his clear-sighted realism and his lack of illusions. But when Decoud finds himself alone on an uninhabited island with the vast load of silver which he and Nostromo had been commissioned to save from the hands of the rebels, he finds his loneliness, unsupported by any idealistic beliefs, unsupportable. "Solitude from mere outward condition of existence becomes very swiftly a state of soul in which the affectations of irony and scepticism have no place. It takes possession of the mind, and drives forth the thought into the exile of utter unbelief. After three days of waiting for the sight of some human face, Decoud caught himself entertaining a

doubt of his own individuality. . . . In our activity alone
do we find the sustaining illusion of an independent existence
as against the whole scheme of things of which we form
a helpless part." Decoud commits suicide. He is in the novel
because Conrad needs his voice, the voice of the ironic and
uncommitted observer of the political scene who nevertheless
finds a satisfaction in acting in that scene and who, when
he ceases to act in it, cannot face the nothingness of his
own isolated self. He in his own way faces the heart of darkness and finds it an intolerable nothingness.

The place of Decoud in the novel is interesting. We
have said that Conrad needed his voice, the voice of the dis-
passionate outsider who sees through the moral pretensions
of both sides. It is Decoud, too, who alone sees right into
Charles Gould's character. Gould's father had had the San
Tomé mine forced on him by a vengeful government official
simply as a means of extorting money from him: it had
been for the father an incubus and a means of persecution.
Gould, haunted by the fact that an unworked mine had been
used as a means of driving his father to a premature death,
determines to return to Costaguana and really make something of the mine; he does so, building it up with the help
of Holroyd, the wealthy American investor, to become the
major factor in the economy of the province and indeed of the
country. He is working for justice, efficiency, stability,
the solvency and international prestige of his country. It
is Gould's (and Holroyd's) money that helps to set up
the Ribiera government:

> In the confidential communications passing between Charles
> Gould, the King of Sulaco, and the head of the silver and
> steel interests far away in California, the conviction was
> growing that any attempt made by men of education and in-

tegrity ought to be discreetly supported. "You may tell your friend Avellanos that I think so," Mr. Holroyd had written at the proper moment from his inviolable sanctuary within the eleven-storey high factory of great affairs. And shortly afterwards, with a credit opened by the Third Southern Bank (located next door but one to the Holroyd Building), the Ribierist party in Costaguana took a practical shape under the eye of the administrator of the San Tomé mine. And Don José, the hereditary friend of the Gould family, could say: "Perhaps, my dear Carlos, I shall not have believed in vain."

The association of Gould, Don José Avellanos, and Mr. Holroyd is in itself a whole epitome of a phase of modern economic history: Gould, scion of a family of British entrepreneurs long settled in the country, who believes in decency and stability; Don José, the passionately patriotic liberal who sees in Gould and his industrial efficiency the opportunity for making his country at last prosperous, free, and respected; and Mr. Holroyd, directing operations from his office in San Francisco. Conrad is not condemning this association; he sometimes shows carefully controlled irony in describing it but absolutely no moral indignation. He goes further and builds up our sympathy for Charles Gould by describing vividly the humiliations to which his father had been subjected by a corrupt and vindictive government and the generous resolution which Charles formed (and communicated to his understanding bride) to undo the past by returning to Costaguana and really making something of the mine. But when Decoud, the uncommitted outsider, looks dispassionately at Charles Gould, he sees the truth about him, which is an important truth about the relation between politics and economics as well as a significant insight into a well-known aspect of the British character. He sees that he is a sentimentalist, as he tells Mrs. Gould, a sentimentalist who "cannot act or exist without idealizing every simple feeling, desire, or achievement. He could not believe his own motives if he did not make them first a part of some fairy tale." Decoud understands that it is Charles Gould's very moral integrity, his determination to do nothing that he cannot find an idealistic motive for, a motive in which he really believes, that makes his interest in the mine so obsessive and in the end so de-humanizing. After Decoud's conversation with Mrs. Gould, we are shown how now she sees the mine as a burden, no longer as the shining opportunity which she had encouraged her husband to grasp when he first talked of it to her, just before they were married. The juxtaposition is important in weaving the pattern of the novel. After Decoud has called Charles a sentimentalist, Mrs. Gould retires to her room and broods on recent events:

> The fate of the San Tomé mine was lying heavy upon her heart. It was a long time now since she had begun to fear it. It had been an idea. She had watched it with misgivings turning into a fetish, and now the fetish had grown into a monstrous and crushing weight. It was as if the inspiration of their early years had left her heart to turn into a wall of silver-bricks, erected by the silent work of evil spirits, between her and her husband. He seemed to dwell alone within a circumvallation of precious metal, leaving her outside with her school, her hospital, the sick mothers and the feeble old men, mere insignificant vestiges of the initial inspiration. "Those poor people!" she murmured to herself.

The last we hear of the people is very near the end of the novel: "The Señor Administrador [Gould] starts for the mountain in an hour. There is some trouble with the workmen to be feared, it appears." Yet Gould had long established himself as a just and conscientious employer. "You have proved yourself a just man," a representative of the people had said to him earlier in the novel. "There had been no wrong doing to any one since you called upon the people to work in the mountains. My brother says that no official of the Government, no oppressor of the Campo, had been seen on your side of the stream. Your own officials do not oppress the people in the gorge. Doubtless they are afraid of your severity. You are a just man and a powerful one." Yet in the end we are left with the feeling that the very importance of the mine in the economic life of the country and in international finance inevitably destroys any satisfactory relationship between employer and employed and produces oppression automatically. "There is no peace and no rest in the development of material interests." But it must be emphasized once again that every alternative shown in the novel is considerably worse than that represented by the combination of sentimentalist and exploiter in the Gould-Holroyd relationship, and the Ribiera government is without question better in every respect than that represented by its opponents. Left and right have little meaning in Conrad's presentation of the situation—and how accurate the presentation is can be seen if we reflect on how little conventional categories of political left and right have been able to fit, say, the situation in Argentina in the 1940's and 1950's. In the end Conrad's voice is very like Decoud's: he sees through everything, but he joins in, though for his own reasons. When he withdraws again, it is to find the isolated and uncommitted life intolerable. Conrad in his later years avoided Decoud's fate by professing the morality of fidelity and honor which he knew was expected of him as a writer of the sea; but the profession did not come from the true depths of his moral imagination. The true logic of his pessimism was too hard.

It is perhaps additional evidence for the affinity between
Decoud and Conrad that (as he tells us in his Author's Note)
the relationship between Decoud and Antonia Avellanos is
modeled on that between Conrad and his own first love.
Not that we must consider the ironical *boulevardier* as in
any way a self-portrait by Conrad; the *boulevardier* is a
heavy disguise; but his voice remains one of Conrad's own
voices. Another voice that is partially Conrad's is that of
Dr. Monygham, disillusioned and embittered by his horrid
sufferings at the hands of the Bento regime, yet still capable
of loyalty (though to a person, no longer to an ideal) and
self-sacrifice.

The variety of voices which tell the story of the novel
are, like the shifts in time and the putting together of the
narrative through a complex pattern of retrospect and contemporaneity, devices to achieve that kind of completeness
and objectivity that we find more often in great drama than
in fiction. If Decoud's voice is partly Conrad's, it is never
presented as such and in the unfolding of the story plays
in fact a less important part than the voice of the fussy,
unimaginative Captain Joseph Mitchell, superintendent in
Sulaco of the Oceanic Steam Navigation Company. Again
and again Captain Mitchell is introduced as telling in retrospect part of the complicated modern history of Costaguana and especially of the western province of Sulaco,
which is the center of the action. He does not understand
what he tells, and his complacent tone and utter lack of
perception provide an almost comic air to much of his
narrative. Yet *we* understand Captain Mitchell, and the result
is that the lack of imagination in his story-telling can sometimes appear as devastating understatement or ironic dead-
pan. He is of course a silly man, yet at the same time ad-

mirable. He is quite fearless, as his behavior when captured and held by the rebel Sotillo in the Custom House reveals. He is completely loyal to his company and to the Goulds. Yet, like Captain MacWhirr in *Typhoon*, his courage is bound up with his lack of imagination, even his lack of understanding. He excites amused laughter, rather than admiration as MacWhirr does, because (except for the moment of crisis with Sotillo, when we *do* admire him in some way) we see him on shore in a routine peacetime job, not in the midst of a typhoon. MacWhirr on shore would have been little different. Both characters find life uncomplicated by moral questions; physical danger is the only threat they recognize and they meet it head on. They can never become Lord Jims, for they have not the imagination, nor Decouds, for they have not the intelligence. They are the type most fit for survival in human society. It is appropriate that such a character should tell much of the complex and basically tragic story of *Nostromo* from the point of view of that impercipience that has most survival value—ironically appropriate, to such a novelist as Conrad. In saying this we must not ignore the profound observation and understanding revealed in the way Conrad makes Mitchell talk: he is an almost Dickensian comic character while at the same time his role in the novel is a much more subtle one than that played by any of Dickens' great comic characters.

As for Nostromo himself, the gallant Capataz de Cargadores, since he gives his name to the novel we might expect him to be the central character in it. This courageous exhibitionist, who lives for reputation, is led by a combination of circumstances to believe that he has been merely exploited by the rich, and this belief, together with his dangerous and politically important mission of taking the silver out to sea away from the clutches of the rebels and the fact that in the end he alone knows where the silver is concealed, leads him to betray his trust and steal the silver. But he too has been betrayed, as he believes and as is in a sense true, for those who have used him have never given the slightest thought to his own real needs and sensibilities. The silver in turn destroys him, for his necessity to "grow rich very slowly," to keep the silver concealed on the island and sell it gradually bit by bit, cuts across his necessities as a gallant lover, and the result is fatal. Nostromo is never, however, a fully realized character. We see him parading on horseback and indulging in histrionic gestures of gallantry or leadership, we hear of his tremendous exploits, his endurance, resourcefulness, prestige; we watch his confidence being disturbed by Monygham's bitterness and Gould's calm irony; we see him finally trapped by the twin forces of love and greed. But we are not wholly convinced. The moment of full reality for Nostromo is when he and Decoud are out with the lighter containing the silver in the impenetrable blackness of the gulf—this is a tremendous scene, one of Conrad's very finest—but both before and after this we are expected to believe what we are told about him rather than allow ourselves to be convinced by the persuasive unfolding of the action. The final section of the novel, with old Giorgio Viola and his two daughters living on the island where the silver is concealed, and Nostromo betrothed to the elder daughter and passionately loving the younger (and loved by both), moves to its tragic climax in a more obviously melodramatic way than the earlier parts of *Nostromo*, and its relation to the main themes of the novel does not seem to be central. It could be plausibly argued that *Nostromo* would be a better novel without its last two chapters, ending with Mrs. Gould's last despairing vision of material interests. Yet Viola could not have been allowed to disappear silently, for his place in the earlier part of the novel, and his relation and that of his wife to Nostromo, were obviously being worked up to some higher pitch of meaning. Viola himself, the old Garibaldino, is a chorus from another world, and Conrad must have felt that a character could not be left alone to act as chorus, he must be integrated somehow into the body of the action. He was probably right, but it is hard to be satisfied that the integration was achieved in a wholly satisfactory way. The novelette with which *Nostromo* ends, though it is convincing enough in its own terms, is on a different level of probability and a lower level of complexity than the bulk of the novel.

The total performance remains nevertheless remarkable. It has been suggested that *Nostromo* lacks a sense of daily living in the texture of its narrative, to which one can only reply that the truth and reality of this South American community and of those who govern its destiny are achieved with such persuasive wholeness that everything else is at once conceded by the reader. And the breaking-up of the narrative, the shifting of times and places and points of view, helps to build up that sense of utter conviction, as though this were not a mere story to be told straight off in a chronological line, but part of the complex pattern of life, which we can look at only through a mixture of retrospect and anticipation, of memory and desire, of the endless intertwining of cause and effect. One is less conscious of *Nostromo* as a work of art, or of artifice, than one is of some of the other novels. But this is the art that conceals art. There is of course an absolute difference between art and life; but if a novel strikes us as being even more historical than history while at the same time containing all the illumination of art, this is a triumph of art, not of simple recording. Aristotle said that tragedy was more philosophical and more serious than history, and this can be said of *Nostromo* with the addition that it is also more convincing as history than history itself. It is history without illusions, written with the tragic calm of desperate knowledge.

Conrad wrote two other novels which are concerned with politics, this time more narrowly and on a far smaller canvas —*The Secret Agent* (1907) and *Under Western Eyes* (1911). Both these novels, though in very different ways, explore aspects of isolation and the impossibility (as well as the necessity) of politics. *The Secret Agent* is in many ways the oddest of all Conrad's stories: its hero, if he can be called a hero, is a man who for the sake of an easy and quiet life makes his living as an agent provocateur employed by the Russian embassy in London. His activities as a supposed anarchist and spy on fellow members of anarchist societies in London have been fatuous rather than spectacular until—and this is where the novel really begins—he is sharply told by the embassy that something striking is required to shock the British government out of its policy of giving refuge to exiled revolutionaries from Russia and elsewhere. The task he is given is to blow up the Greenwich Observatory. With the help of his wife's idiot brother, who of course has no idea of what he is supposed to be doing, he tries to do this, but the result is that the idiot brother-in-law stumbles with the explosives and blows himself up, without doing any further harm. Verloc's wife, who had married him for security and to achieve a home for her beloved young brother, is rudely jerked out of her torpid acceptance of a satisfactory domestic routine by her brother's

death and particularly by her husband's casually apologetic
way of reporting it, and in a fit of brutal anger and revulsion
stabs Verloc with a carving knife just when he imagines
that a cozy and amorous reconciliation is about to take
place. Mrs. Verloc in desperation then appeals to one of her
husband's friends (an anarchist whom Mr. Verloc had been
cultivating for professional reasons) to take her away, but,
having put her on the boat train at Waterloo Station, he slips
away and leaves her to cross the Channel alone. She commits
suicide by throwing herself from the boat in mid-Channel.

The plot itself, thus baldly summarized, shows an almost
ghoulish imagination, and indeed there is a coldly savage
irony throughout this book which shows Conrad's imagination working in a curiously disturbed manner. The invention
of Verloc himself, with his laziness and his impassiveness,
is a remarkable feat, and scarcely less remarkable is the
picture of the Verloc ménage and the way of life that acts
itself out with satisfactory resignation behind the stationer's
and newsagent's shop which is Verloc's legitimate business
and his "front." Stevie, Mrs. Verloc's young brother, is
an attempt at a portrait of a holy idiot in almost Dostoevskian
terms, but the holiness is not really achieved and we have
a sense only of confused and nearly mindless compassion
with all suffering both animal and human. Stevie is thus
a parallel to the various revolutionaries who are portrayed
in the book, but like them he is not shown as a real person
whose attitudes and plans can be taken seriously. The politics
of desperation and the politics of mindless compassion are
equally meaningless and ineffective, while on the other side
the politics of tyranny and terror, against which the anarchists
are in revolt, are shown as both cruel and absurd. Between
the two stand the English police, civilized and moderate,

but not equipped by either intellect or imagination to understand anarchists and similar political rebels. Chief Inspector
Heat understood burglars. "They were his fellow-citizens
gone wrong because of imperfect education, Chief Inspector
Heat believed: but allowing for that difference, he could
understand the mind of a burglar, because, as a matter
of fact, the mind and the instincts of a burglar are of the
same kind as the mind and the instincts of a police officer. . . .
Products of the same machine, one classed as useful and the
other as noxious, they take the machine for granted in different ways, but with a seriousness essentially the same. The
mind of Chief Inspector Heat was inaccessible to ideas
of revolt." And when the Assistant Commissioner talks
of the bomb plot to the Home Secretary, the latter, in
his continual insistence that the Assistant Commissioner
must explain the situation lucidly, briefly, and in a manner
consistent with the Home Secretary's own preconceived
notions, reflects Conrad's irony even here.

But the most disturbing parts of the book are not those
dealing with the anarchists and their ideas—Conrad's contempt for them is too great for him to take them seriously,
and they are mere caricatures—but with the Verlocs and
their nest of domestic tranquillity and even in a sense felicity,
whose unreality is only demonstrated in the final crisis.
This little domestic society, with its familiar routine, its
satisfactory mutual adjustments, its devices for pandering
to the secret needs of each one of its members, seems to
work and actually does work until it is forced apart in the
most violent way by the sudden revelation of those secret
needs. Mrs. Verloc had been a good wife, attentive, patient,
content to let her husband go off on unexplained business
whenever he needed to without asking questions and with

what appeared utter trust. Verloc in his way had been
a good husband. But Mrs. Verloc's only real affection was
for her idiot brother, to whom her husband gave a home,
and Mr. Verloc's only real affection was for himself. The
bomb crisis suddenly exposed that, though Verloc's massive
self-love makes him blind to the reality of his wife's state
almost up to the very moment of her plunging the knife
into him. The murder takes place after he has tried his
final (and he thinks successful) means of pacifying her
indignation at his having virtually murdered her brother:
" 'Come here,' he said in a peculiar tone, which might have
been the tone of brutality, but was intimately known to
Mrs. Verloc as the note of wooing." She goes to him, but
holding the knife. It is an ugly and powerful scene, and
references to marital intimacy in such a context have the
effect of destroying the whole concept, of suggesting that
all such intimacy is both illusory and squalid. The great
society, which has already been shown to be either terrible
or crazy or based on incomprehension, is reduced at the
end of the novel to the little society, which is both terrible
and crazy and incomprehensible. That Mr. Verloc is an
agent provocateur working for Czarist Russia against anarchists in England, that the mediating factor between his
public and his private life is the compassionate idiot Stevie,
and that the economic security he gives (until the climax)
to his wife and brother-in-law is the result of his tragicomi-
cally inept spying and plotting, are facts that relate to each
other only through an irony so aloof, so savagely withdrawn,
that the reader cannot help wondering whether Conrad
in writing this novel was more concerned to reveal something
or to suppress something.

There is withdrawal, too, in *Under Western Eyes*. This

story of a lonely Russian student, illegitimate son of a nobleman with no known relatives or close friends, who works ambitiously at his studies until his whole life is suddenly changed by a political assassin's taking refuge in his lodgings, is presented as a story incredible to Western eyes, as something that could only happen to Russians. It is told by an elderly English teacher of languages in Geneva, who has come into possession of the hero's diary, and who frequently emphasizes how different the Western mind is. Conrad's distancing of the story is partly again an ironic device and partly, one suspects, a way of suppressing or at least deflecting the anti-Russian feelings which this son of an ardent Polish nationalist had been brought up with. Conrad also, who professed to hate Dostoevsky, is here writing his most Dostoevskian novel which has been clearly influenced by the Russian novelist; perhaps this is a further reason for withdrawing himself from his story.

The student Razumov, when he finds the fugitive revolutionary in his room, is caught in an impossible dilemma. Whatever he does now—whether he helps him or denounces him—the pattern of his life has been destroyed. Razumov, though he is well aware of the excesses of Russian tyranny and wishes for a more liberal government, has no use for revolutionary violence or utopian assassins. This lonely man had thought to stake a claim in Russia by winning an academic reputation for himself and ending his life as a distinguished Russian professor. But when the student Haldin, having just killed a particularly vicious and tyrannical Russian official (together with a number of innocent bystanders), comes to Razumov for help under the mistaken impression that Razumov's withdrawn silence in his classes denoted his trustworthy revolutionary character, Razumov sees this possibility disappear at once. Conrad gives an immensely forceful picture of his inward rage and frustration as Haldin lies on his bed and talks to him as to a fellow conspirator. He is absolutely trapped, and trapped in something from which he had wished to keep himself free, uncommitted to either side, pursuing his own lonely career. He consents to carry a message from Haldin to a sledge-driver to arrange for Haldin to be picked up and driven to a distant railway station—that is the only way he can get him out of his room. But he finds the driver dead drunk and insensible; he thrashes him in a fit of hysterical rage, then returns home in the snow, but on the way he decides that the only thing to do now is to denounce Haldin to the authorities. This he does before returning to his lodgings, and Haldin eventually leaves, to go to certain capture and death. But Razumov's life is not restored to its former tranquillity. After days of alternating anguish and listlessness he is summoned before Councillor Mikulin, who conducts an inquisition both friendly and terrifying—a masterly scene. It ends with Razumov asking leave to retire:

". . . To retire—simply to retire," he finished with great resolution.

He walked to the door, thinking, "Now he must show his hand. He must ring and have me arrested before I am out of the building, or he must let me go. And either way. . . ."

An unhurried voice said—

"Kirylo Sidorovitch."

Razumov at the door turned his head.

"To retire," he repeated.

"Where to?" asked Councillor Mikulin softly.

This question echoes through the book. For indeed Razumov has been caught up in a commitment from which there can be no retiral. Haldin's friends regard him as one of Haldin's fellow conspirators. The government knows this, and also knows that he is not in fact a revolutionary. In the end he finds himself inevitably led to agree to Mikulin's proposal that he act as a government spy on Russian revolutionary exiles in Geneva.

So Razumov moves from loneliness to a set of false social relationships. Before, he had to face the problem of living and working alone; now he has to face the far more difficult problem of acting out a continuous lie in relation to the people he meets. For in Geneva he has to associate with exiled Russians who hail him as a hero for having taken part in the assassination committed by Haldin. His most testing relationship is with Natalia Haldin, sister of the now executed Haldin, who sees in him her only contact with her adored brother and is ready to hero-worship him. She alone of all the Russians in Geneva is treated with respect and admiration; her faith is pure and genuine and her hope is for a regenerated Russia in which both revolutionaries and tyrants will be forgotten in a new social concord. The continuous acting of a lie is discovered by Razumov to be a peculiarly excruciating form of loneliness. (Earlier, before he had left Russia, he had already grown to welcome his interviews with Mikulin because with him alone he could take for granted knowledge of the truth of his relations with Haldin.) The account of the other Geneva Russians, exiled revolutionaries, is highly ironical and uncomplimentary, and Razumov's contempt for their chief figure increases his self-hate in acting his part before them and at the same time accentuates the tone of self-defensive irony in which he feels bound to talk to them. This tone misleads some into thinking him a dedicated and lonely man of action, while others are puzzled. But none is really suspicious, though Razumov keeps thinking that they might be. If this group is portrayed with irony and even at times with contempt, Conrad nevertheless portrays them with a seriousness which he did not accord to the anarchists in *The Secret Agent*. In his portrait of Sophia Antonovna he even shows a reluctant admiration for her dedicated commitment to revolutionary action. The revolutionaries as shown by Conrad are credible people whose conversation and behavior reveal the inevitable link between idealism and vanity, the inevitable claims of the self on society. Razumov in the end is redeemed beyond self, and at the same time beyond any possibility of a social life. He is driven by inner compulsion to confess the truth before the Geneva revolutionaries, and after being badly beaten and having his eardrums broken by one of them who himself turns out later to have been a police spy, he is taken under the protection of an abused and exploited woman servant of the chief Geneva revolutionary, and she takes him back to Russia to tend his broken body during the few years that remain to him.

The resolution is desperate, made possible only by the genuine selflessness, the positive sainthood, of Razumov's rescuer. It is not a resolution, even on the most symbolic level, of the problems posed by the novel. The man who, like Conrad himself, understands both sides of the tyrant-terrorist struggle, sees the moral and intellectual defects of both and so refuses to commit himself to either, is trapped into commitment. His neutrality traps him. But it is not a real commitment; it involves a lie in the soul; and the only way out of *that* is virtual self-destruction. Put thus bluntly, the theme of *Under Western Eyes* seems despairing indeed. But the texture of the novel introduces other levels of significance which, while not suggesting more adequate solutions, at least set going rhythms of compassion and simple honesty which somehow make the human world of the novel less negative. There is grim humor in some of the dialogue, as well as bitter irony and searching analysis. Simple sainthood is the last positive ideal which emerges, but it is never shown as anything other than a last refuge of harassed simplicity. It will not do for the others. And all the time Conrad feels it necessary to reassure us by saying that this is not *our* world: this is the West looking at the mysterious East. But we see through the pretense: this is not a novel about the inscrutable Slav soul, but about the fate of political man.

In emphasizing the themes of self and society in Conrad we must not be taken to deny the magnificence of some of his sea stories or the brilliance of the detail with which he can present tales of sailors and adventurers. Some of these tales—"The Shadow Line," for example, a splendid story, both meticulously realistic and profoundly symbolic, of an initiatory testing experience at sea, or "The Secret Sharer," a story of an incident in a young captain's first command told with a quiet precision which both localizes it in time and place with absolute conviction and at the same time expands it into a central clue for an understanding of much of Conrad, or *Typhoon*, which has what is perhaps the finest account of a storm in English literature—show his genius working with perfect assurance. Yet he himself became impatient with those critics who considered him as primarily a writer of sea stories, and we can understand why. He used what he knew, and knew uniquely among English novelists, in order to probe an aspect of the human dilemma which is not confined to sailors, and when he had exhausted his sea knowledge in his fiction he moved on to find other ways of exploring paradoxes of human values as revealed in loneliness and in community.

4

"Dubliners"

James Joyce left his native Dublin at the age of twenty-two, and lived ever after in self-imposed exile on the Continent. Yet all his work is concerned with Dublin; his characters are Dubliners, his background is Dublin, his atmosphere is Dublin, and all the tremendous resources of his symbolic realism were employed in creating in language the essence and reality of the Dublin he turned his back on as a young man. This fact is in itself symbolic. Joyce's literary career was a progressive attempt to insulate himself against the life which is his subject as an artist until he reached the point at which what one may call ideal comedy became possible. There are many definitions of comedy, but the definition that is most relevant to a consideration of such a work as *Ulysses* as comedy is that which identifies the comic spirit with the author's renunciation of any share in the world he portrays. Tragedy and comedy, insofar as they arise from differences in attitude, differ essentially on this point. Comedy is written by one who, temporarily or permanently, has renounced his share in human destiny; tragedy is the work of one who is all too conscious of his share. Indeed, the same story may be comic or tragic according to whether the arrangement and emphasis of the events result in stressing or in minimizing the author's (and so, for the critic, the reader's) sense of community with the life he creates. The failure of Hamlet to cope with the circumstances in the midst of which he finds himself is tragic because those circumstances are presented as part of the author's world, of our world:[1] it would be comic if the details of style and organization were handled so as to insulate author and reader from any such community and the theme became an intellectual one of frustration—the theme of most comedies. The theme of *Ulysses*—if we can differentiate the theme from the treatment—is in itself neither comic nor tragic; but it is presented with the supreme aloofness that makes supreme comedy. Joyce leaves Ireland in order to write about Ireland; he shuns the life which is his subject in order to be able to embody that life in his art as an artist only and not as a fellow countryman or even as a fellow mortal. So the main fact about Joyce's biography has a direct connection with the main fact about his art—the fact that *Ulysses* (and, though with obvious differences, *Finnegans Wake*) constitute comedy at its ultimate point.

Joyce's work, however, is not so homogeneous that such an explanation can fit all of it. It fits *Dubliners* only to a limited extent (and *Dubliners* was written while Joyce was still in Dublin) and it does not fit *A Portrait of the Artist as a Young Man* at all. The road to the renunciation that produced *Ulysses* and *Finnegans Wake* was not a straight one. In *Dubliners* Joyce is simply the clear-eyed observer, and he is observing what is around him, so that these stories have none of the symbolizing qualities that memory lends. *A Portrait of the Artist* is a work of exorcism. Joyce seems to have decided that until he had come to terms with the life

---

[1] Not, of course, on the physical level.

which had molded him he would not be free to embody that life in his art. He grapples directly with himself considered as a product of his environment; in doing so he attains complete self-consciousness about the process he is describing; and so henceforth he can defy determinism—he has faced the problem squarely and won the right to dismiss it. He has shaped his own connection with Ireland into a work of art and has exorcised the evil spirit of self-consciousness—that spirit which has such an inhibiting influence on the production of comedy. Exorcism or catharsis, *A Portrait of the Artist* certainly enabled Joyce to get certain inhibiting forces out of his system, and by doing so made *Ulysses* possible.

There are thus four periods in Joyce's life as a writer. First, the period of *Dubliners* where he gives us thumbnail sketches of characteristic situations of the life of which he is still a part, in spite of the studied objectivity of his approach. Joyce is a part of the Ireland of *Dubliners* in the same dim way that Chekhov is a part of the Russia he presents in his plays and stories. The second period, producing the autobiographical *Portrait*, is one of candid study of his relation to the forces that have made him, with the gradual realization of the impossibility of his remaining longer in such an environment if he was to achieve that kind of artistic integrity which he had already set for himself as his aim. The third period, to which the conclusion of the *Portrait* had so directly pointed, follows; the period when he is free to re-create in language, on both the realistic and the symbolic levels, the life he had renounced, making that renunciation as the price he deemed necessary for artistic integrity and the objectivity of true comedy, but conscious of the risk involved in thus severing his ties with that microcosm of civilization which had produced him and which for him stood for humanity.

Stephen tells Cranly toward the end of *A Portrait:*

> ". . . I do not fear to be alone or to be spurned for another or to leave whatever I have to leave. And I am not afraid to make a mistake, even a great mistake, and perhaps as long as eternity too."
>
> Cranly, now grave again, slowed his pace and said:
>
> "Alone, quite alone. You have no fear of that. And you know what that word means? Not only to be separate from all others but to have not even one friend."
>
> "I will take the risk," said Stephen.

Ulysses was produced as the result of Joyce's having taken that risk.

The fourth period produced *Finnegans Wake.* Here Joyce created in a purely symbolic manner an epitome of the life he renounced, rejecting the realistic narrative basis on which *Ulysses* was organized and enlarging the symbolic element to include both theme and technique, and further to the point where it involves interfering with the very English language itself. From one point of view at least, it marks the completion of Joyce's journey from realism to symbolism.

Let us now turn back to *Dubliners* and consider in more detail the nature of Joyce's achievement here. The short stories that make up this book have certain common features in aim and technique; they are realistic in a certain sense, and they have a quite extraordinary evenness of tone and texture, the style being that neutral medium which, without in itself showing any signs of emotion or excitement, conveys with quiet adequacy the given story in its proper atmosphere and with its proper implications. Only the last story in the collection, "The Dead," stands apart from the others; here Joyce has done something different—he has presented a story in a way that implies comment, and he has deliberately allowed his style to surrender, as it were, to that comment, so that the level objectivity of the other stories is replaced by a more lyrical quality.

The first three stories are told in the first person, the principle of selection, which determines the choice, organization, and emphasis of the incidents, being provided by the recollected impressions of the narrator. Thus, in "The Sisters" Joyce gives the constituent parts of what, to a sensitive boy, made up (whether actually or not is irrelevant) a single and memorable experience; and these parts are arranged and patterned in such a way as to give a sense of the unity of the experience to the reader. And although it is irrelevant to the critic whether the events actually occurred or not, it is very relevant that the pattern of events should be one which produces a recognizable experience with its attendant atmosphere. A purely "formal" analysis of any of these stories would be useful—in fact, indispensable—in an endeavor to assess their value as literature, but such an analysis is only the first step in a process; it is not in itself able to tell us why that particular arrangement of incident and description constitutes a totality which has more value than a mere symmetrical pattern or intriguing design. The arrangement of events in "The Sisters" or "Araby" produces a good short story because the result is not merely a pattern *qua* pattern (such has no *necessary* value in literature), but a pattern which corresponds to something in experience. For those who, owing to the circumstances of their life or the limitations of their sensibility, are unable to recognize that correspondence, the story loses most of its worth: there is always this limitation to the universality of great literature, this stumbling-block to the purely formal critical approach. A study of *Dubliners* can tell us a great deal about the function of pattern in fiction and about the relation between realism as a technique and as an end. No English short-story writer has built up his design, has related the parts to the preconceived whole, more carefully than Joyce has done in stories such as "The Sisters," "Two Gallants," or "Ivy Day in the Committee Room." Observation is the tool of imagination, and imagination is that which can see potential significance in the most casual seeming events. It is the more specifically and consciously artistic faculty that organizes, arranges, balances emphases, and sets going undercurrents of symbolic comment, until that potential significance has become actual.

In the second of these stories, "An Encounter," the organizing and selecting principle is again the boy's impressionable mind and memory as recalled or conceived by Joyce. It is worth noting how Joyce sets the pattern going in this and other stories. Descriptive comment concerning the chief characters constitutes the opening paragraph—comment that wanders to and fro in its tenses, not starting with a clear edge of incident but with a jagged line, as though memory were gradually searching out those events which really were the beginning of the design which is a totality in the retrospective mind. Similarly, in "The Sisters," the opening paragraph consists of an almost regular alternation of imperfect and pluperfect tenses:

> Night after night I had passed the house . . . and studied the lighted square of window. . . . If he was dead, I thought, I would see the reflection of candles on the darkened blind.
> . . He had often said to me: "I am not long for this world," and I had thought his words idle. Now I knew they were true. . . .

These deliberately wavering beginnings serve a double function. First, they give the author an opportunity of presenting to the reader any preliminary information that is necessary to his understanding of the story; they enable him, too, to let out those pieces of information in the order which will give them most significance and throw the necessary amount of emphasis onto what the author wishes to be emphasized. Second, on a simple, naturalistic level they give us the pattern of an experience as it actually is to memory or observation. The beginning is vague (the reader should study the evidence of witnesses in reports of court trials to understand how wavering the beginning of a unified experience is to both observer and sufferer), but once under way the jagged line becomes straight, until the end, which is precise and definite. Our own memories of experiences which have been significant for us will provide sufficient comment on this technique. In those stories which are told in the first person, as memories, the jagged-line openings are more conspicuous than in the stories narrated in the third person: Joyce has not done this accidentally.

Very different are the conclusions of the stories. A series of events is recognized as having constituted a totality, a "significant experience," in virtue of its close, not of its opening. The conclusions of these stories are level and precise, the last lines denoting a genuine climax of realization (if told in the first person) or in the pattern of the objective situation (if told in the third). And the pause is genuine. If the reader were taken on five minutes farther he might find the addition unnecessary or silly, but it would not cancel out the effect of the whole story, as the prolongation of the trick conclusions of so many modern short-story writers would. In many of O. Henry's short stories, for example, where the final point is contained in a fraction of a moment sustained in print simply by the author's refusing to go farther, the conclusion is not a genuine one, no real end to a pattern, but simply a piece of wit on the author's part. The stories they tell are not real patterns or wholes but are made to appear so only by the epigrammatic form of the conclusion, and the point would be lost if the author told his readers the succeeding event. Joyce is not in this tradition—he has more respect for his art. His final pauses are as genuine as the final bars of a Beethoven symphony, though not nearly so obvious. The degeneration of the short story—and the short stage play, too—into the extended epigram was a feature of the 1920's and 1930's. Perhaps it is due to some extent to the influence of the curtain stage, where the author is absolved from the necessity of creating a genuine conclusion by the rapid descent of the curtain, cutting off the audience from the stage at a single stroke. The platform stage of the Elizabethans encouraged healthier tendencies: there the end of the pattern had to be real, the pause a real pause, for there was no slick curtain to relieve the writer of his responsibility. Genuine pause does not imply a long-drawn-out conclusion or an uneconomical art: Joyce's endings are subtle and rapid:

"What do you think of that, Crofton," cried Mr. Henchy.
"Isn't that fine? What?"
Mr. Crofton said that it was a very fine piece of writing.

Or:

Gazing up into the darkness I saw myself as a creature driven and derided by vanity; and my eyes burned with anguish and anger.

And there is the immensely subtle and effective ending of "Grace," concluding in the middle of Father Purdon's sermon. The platform-stage ending does not require verbosity or obviousness; it requires only that the last line shall really conclude the pattern; that the reader's pause shall be real and not forced on him by a trick of the author in refusing to say more when there is more to be said,

"Two Gallants," a gray, unexciting incident whose predominant mood is illustrated by the setting—late Sunday evening in a deserted street of Dublin—is one of Joyce's minor triumphs. It is a perfect example of the organization of the casual until, simply by the order and relation of the parts, it becomes significant, not only a sordid incident that happened at a given moment but a symbol of a type of civilization. The arrangement of detail so as to give the utmost density to the narrative is a striking quality here, as it is in "Ivy Day in the Committee Room." Joyce will pause to elaborate the description of a character at a certain point of the story, and it is only by a careful, critical analysis that we appreciate the full effect of having that pause in that place and in no other. Always the location of particularizing detail is such that it suggests the maximum amount of implication. In "Ivy Day in the Committee Room" two features of Joyce's technique are dominant: first, every action is symbolic of the atmosphere he wishes to create, and, second, the pauses for description are carefully arranged and balanced so as to emphasize the symbolic nature of the action. The introduction of candles to light up the bareness of the room at the particular point in the story when Joyce wishes to draw the reader's attention to its bareness is one of many examples:

> A denuded room came into view and the fire lost all its cheerful colour. The walls of the room were bare except for a copy of an election address. In the middle of the room was a small table on which papers were heaped.

A simple enough piece of description, but it has been held back till now and allowed to emerge naturally as a result of the candle incident at a point where the emphasis on bareness,

on the loss of the fire's cheerful color, and on the dreary un-
tidiness of the room, gains its maximum effect as regards
both structure and atmosphere. Similarly, the manipulation
of the Parnell motif in this story shows great skill. It is suggested in the title, but does not break through to the surface
of the story until, at a point carefully chosen by Joyce, Mr.
Hynes takes off his coat, "displaying, as he did so, an ivy
leaf in the lapel." And henceforth this motif winds in and out
until its culmination in Mr. Hynes's recitation. And no
more effective symbol of the relation between two of the
main interests of Dubliners in the beginning of this century
has ever been created than in this simple, realistic piece of
dialogue and description:

> "This is Parnell's anniversary," said Mr. O'Connor, "and
> don't let us stir up any bad blood. We all respect him now
> that he's dead and gone—even the Conservatives," he added,
> turning to Mr. Crofton.
> Pok! The tardy cork flew out of Mr. Crofton's bottle. Mr.
> Crofton got up from his box and went to the fire. As he re-
> turned with his capture he said in a deep voice:
> "Our side of the house respects him because he was a
> gentleman."

The claims of liquor impinge naturally on those of politics,
as anyone who has seen a certain section of the Scottish
Nationalists at work in Edinburgh today can well understand. A similar point is made in Mr. Kernan's remark in
"Grace."

> " 'Course he is," said Mr. Kernan, "and a damned decent
> Orangeman, too. We went into Butler's in Moore Street—
> faith I was genuinely moved, tell you the God's truth—and I
> remember well his very words. *Kernan*, he said, *we worship at
> different altars*, he said, *but our belief is the same*. Struck me as
> very well put."

This time it is religion and liquor that mingle so effortlessly. The slipping-in of the name of the bar right beside Mr. Kernan's expression of his genuine religious emotion is realistic and convincing in itself and is also symbolic in that it makes, thus economically, a point about the Irish character.

Joyce's realism in *Dubliners* is not therefore the casual observation of the stray photographer, nor is it the piling-up of unrelated details. All the stories are deliberately and carefully patterned, all have a density, a fulness of implication, which the even tone of the narrative by disguising only renders more effective. The almost terrifying calm of "An Encounter," the aloof recording of "Eveline," the hard clarity of carefully ordered detail in "After the Race," the carefully balanced interiors in "A Little Cloud," the penetrating climax of "Counterparts," the quiet effectiveness of "Clay" —to select only some of the more obvious points—are the work of an artist whose gift of observation, tremendous as it is, is never allowed to thwart his literary craftsmanship—his ability to construct, arrange, organize. The two most impressive stories in the collection are "Ivy Day in the Committee Room" and the concluding story, "The Dead." The former has in a high degree all the qualities we have noted; it is as careful a piece of patterned realism as any writer has given us. But "The Dead" differs both in theme and technique from all the other stories in *Dubliners* and deserves some discussion to itself.

In "The Dead" Joyce uses a much more expansive technique than he does elsewhere in *Dubliners*. He is not here merely concerned with shaping a series of events into a unity; he has a specific point to make—a preconceived theme in terms of which the events in "The Dead" are selected and arranged. In the other stories there is no point other than the pattern that emerges from his telling of the story; no argument can be isolated and discussed as the "theme" of the story, for the story is the theme and the theme is the story. The insight of the artist organizes the data provided by observation into a totality, but no external principle determines that organization; the principle of organization is determined simply by further contemplation of the data themselves. But "The Dead" is the working-out, in terms of realistic narrative, of a preconceived theme, and that theme is a man's withdrawal into the circle of his own egotism, a number of external factors trying progressively to break down the walls of that circle, and those walls being finally broken down by the culminating assault on his egotism coming simultaneously from without, as an incident affecting him, and from within, as an increase of understanding. Only when we have appreciated this theme does the organization of the story become intelligible to us. On the surface it is the story of Gabriel returning from a jolly time at a party given by his aunts in a mood of desire for his wife and the frustration of that desire on his learning that a song sung by one of the guests at the party had reminded his wife of a youth who had been in love with her many years ago and who had died of pneumonia caught through standing outside her window in the cold and the rain; so that his wife is thinking of that past, in which Gabriel had no share, when he was expecting her to be giving herself to him, the final result being that Gabriel loses his mood of desire and falls asleep in a mood of almost impersonal understanding. But about three-quarters of the story is taken up with a vivid and detailed account of the party, and on first reading the story we are puzzled to know why Joyce devotes so much care and space to the party if the ending is to be simply Gabriel's change of mood on learning how his wife is really feeling. As a piece of simple patterning the story seems lopsided; we have to discover the central theme before we realize how perfectly proportioned the story is.

The theme of the story is the assault on the walled circle of Gabriel's egotism. The first character we see is Lily, the caretaker's daughter, rushed almost off her feet in the performance of her various duties. Then comes a pause, and Joyce turns to describe the Misses Morkan, who are giving the party, and the nature of the function. Then, when this retrospect had been brought up to the time of the opening of the story, Gabriel and his wife enter—late for the party, everyone expecting them. The external environment is drawn first before Gabriel enters and makes it merely an environment for himself. Lily is an independent personality, quite outside Gabriel's environment; she is introduced before Gabriel in order that when Gabriel arrives the reader should be able to feel the contrast between the environment as Gabriel feels it to be (a purely personal one), and as it is to a quite objective observer—the caretaker's daughter to whom the party is just an increase of work. Gabriel is greeted as he enters with a great deal of fuss; he enters naturally into the environment his aunts are preparing for him, but immediately after the greeting he has an illuminating encounter with Lily. He patronizes her, as he had known her since she was a child. He remarks gaily that one of these days he will be going to her wedding. Lily resents the remark and replies bitterly that "the men that is now is only all palaver and what they can get out of you."

What part does this little incident play in the story? It is the first attempt to break down the circle of Gabriel's egotism. He has questioned Lily, not with any sincere desire to learn about her, but in order to indulge his own expansive mood. He does not recognize that Lily and her world exist in their own right; to him they are merely themes for his genial conversation. Gabriel colors at Lily's reply; his egotism is hurt ever so slightly, but the fortress is still very far from taken. How slight the breach was is illustrated by his subsequent action—he thrusts a coin into the girl's hand, warming himself in the glow of his own generosity and not concerned with finding a method of giving that will obviate any embarrassment on Lily's part. On thinking over his encounter with Lily he sees it simply as a failure on his part to take up the right tone, and this failure of his own hurts his pride a little and makes him wonder whether he ought not to change the speech he has prepared for after dinner—perhaps that is the wrong tone too. He sees the whole incident from a purely egotistical point of view; Lily exists only as an excuse for his gesturing, and he is worried lest his gestures are not those which will get most appreciation from his audience.

Then we have Gabriel again in his relation with his aunts. He was always their favorite nephew, we are told. We see his possessive attitude to Gretta, his wife. We see him patting his tie reassuringly when his wife shows a tendency to laugh at him. When that tendency is manifested by Aunt Julia as well he shows signs of anger, and tactful Aunt Kate changes the conversation. The picture of Gabriel as withdrawn behind the walls of his own egotism is carefully built up.

The second assault on Gabriel's egotism is made by Miss Ivors, the Irish Nationalist, who attacks his individualism and asks what he is doing for his people and his country. She succeeds in making Gabriel very uncomfortable, and when she leaves him he tries to banish all thought of the conversation from his memory with the reflection that "of course the girl, or woman, or whatever she was, was an enthusiast but there was a time for all things." He goes on to reflect that "she had tried to make him ridiculous before people, heckling him and staring at him with her rabbit's eyes." And so fails the second attempt to break down the circle of Gabriel's egotism.

Then we see Gabriel in a more congenial atmosphere, where his egotism is safe. He is asked to carve the goose—as usual. But Gabriel has been upset, and his cold refusal of a request by Gretta shows his egotism on the defensive. He runs over the heads of his speech in his mind. It must be changed—changed in such a way as to squash these assaults that are being made on his ego. And so he thinks up a nice, cozy talk about hospitality and humor and humanity and the virtues of the older generation (with which, as against the generation represented by Miss Ivors, he temporarily identifies himself). Eventually the meal begins, and Gabriel takes his seat at the head of the table, thoroughly at ease at last.

Mr. Bartell D'Arcy is Gabriel's counterpart—a figure merely sketched, to serve the part of a symbol in the story. There is deliberate irony on Joyce's part in making Gretta refer to him as conceited in an early conversation with Gabriel. When at dinner a group of guests are discussing with their hostesses the singers of Ireland, their complacency is such as to dismiss Caruso almost with contempt: they had hardly heard of him. Only D'Arcy suggests that Caruso might be better than any of the singers mentioned, and his suggestion is met with skepticism. D'Arcy alone of the guests refuses to drink either port or sherry until persuaded by nudges and whispers. And it is D'Arcy who sings the song that removes Gretta to another world.

Gabriel's speech takes place as planned, and for some

time he revels happily in the little world of which he is the
center. The party ends and the guests stand with coats on in
the hall, about to take their leave. Gabriel is waiting for
Gretta to get ready, and as he and others are waiting the
sound of someone playing the piano comes down to the hall:

> "Who's playing up there?" asked Gabriel.
> "Nobody. They're all gone."
> "O no, Aunt Kate," said Mary Jane. "Bartell D'Arcy and
> Miss O'Callaghan aren't gone yet."
> "Someone is fooling at the piano anyhow," said Gabriel.

D'Arcy is first "nobody"; then—and it is significant for
the structure of the story that it is Gabriel who says this—he
is "fooling at the piano." While Gabriel, a little disturbed
again, is making a final effort to re-establish his full sense of
his own importance by telling a humorous story to the circle
in the hall and thus becoming again the center of attraction,
the sound of someone singing comes downstairs, and Gabriel
sees his wife listening, standing near the top of the first flight
"as if she were a symbol of something." D'Arcy stops
abruptly on being discovered (again the contrast with Gabriel) and finally Gabriel and Gretta set out for the hotel
where they are to spend the night, as it is too far to go home
at such an hour.

Then comes the climax, when the fortified circle of Gabriel's egotism is battered down by a series of sharp blows.
Just at the moment of his greatest self-confidence and desire
for her, Gretta tells him that she is thinking about the song
D'Arcy had sung. He questions her, first genially, and then,
as he begins to realize the implications of the song for Gretta,
more and more coldly:

> "I am thinking about a person long ago who used to sing
> that song."

"And who was the person long ago?"asked Gabriel, smiling.

"It was a person I used to know in Galway when I was living with my grandmother," she said.

The smile passed away from Gabriel's face. . . .

Miss Ivor had talked about Galway; it was one of the symbols of that world of otherness against which Gabriel had been shutting himself in all evening. This is the beginning of the final assault. Then Gabriel learns that the "person" was a young boy that Gretta used to know, long before she knew him. He had been in love with her, and they used to go out walking together. With cold irony Gabriel asks whether that was the reason that Gretta had earlier in the evening expressed a desire to go to Galway for the summer holidays. When she tells him that the young man is dead—dying long since, when he was only seventeen—this line of defense is taken away from Gabriel and he falls back onto his final line:

"What was he?" asked Gabriel, still ironically.

"He was in the gasworks," she said.

Gabriel felt humiliated by the failure of his irony and by the evocation of this figure from the dead, a boy in the gasworks.

Gabriel has no further defenses left. He burns with shame, seeing himself

as a ludicrous figure, acting as a pennyboy for his aunts, a nervous, well-meaning sentimentalist, orating to vulgarians and idealising his own clownish lusts, the pitiable fatuous figure he had caught a glimpse of in the mirror. Instinctively he turned his back more to the light lest she might see the shame that burned upon his forehead.

The full realization that his wife had all along been dwelling in another world, a world he had never entered and of which

he knew nothing, and the utter failure of his irony to bring
his wife back to the world of which he, Gabriel, was the center, finally broke the walled circle of his egotism. A dead
youth, a mere memory, was the center of the world in which
Gretta had all this while been living. As a result of this
knowledge, and the way it has been conveyed, Gabriel es-
capes from himself, as it were, and the rest of the story shows
us his expanding consciousness until the point where, dozing
off into unconsciousness, he feels a sense of absolute unity,
of identity even, with all those elements which before had
been hostile to his ego:

> Generous tears filled Gabriel's eyes. . . . The tears gath-
> ered more thickly in his eyes and in the partial darkness he
> imagined he saw the form of a young man standing under a
> dripping tree. . . . His own identity was fading out into a
> grey impalpable world: the solid world itself, which these
> dead had one time reared and lived in, was dissolving and
> dwindling.
>
> A few light taps upon the pane made him turn to the win-
> dow. It had begun to snow again. He watched sleepily the
> flakes, silver and dark, falling obliquely against the lamplight.
> The time had come for him to set out on his journey west-
> ward. Yes, the newspapers were right: snow was general
> all over Ireland. It was falling on every part of the dark cen-
> tral plain, on the treeless hills, falling softly upon the bog of
> Allen and, further westward, softly falling into the dark
> mutinous Shannon waves. It was falling, too, upon every part
> of the lonely churchyard where Michael Furey lay buried.
> It lay thickly drifted on the crooked crosses and headstones,
> on the spears of the little gate, on the barren thorns. His soul
> swooned slowly as he heard the snow falling faintly through
> the universe and faintly falling, like the descent of their last
> end, upon all the living and the dead.

The snow, which falls indifferently upon all things, covering them with a neutral whiteness and erasing all their differentiating details, is the symbol of Gabriel's new sense of identity with the world, of the breakdown of the circle of his egotism to allow him to become for the moment not a man different from all other men living in a world of which he alone is the center but a willing part of the general flux of things. The assault, which progressed through so many stages until its final successful stage, had this result, and the contrast with the normal Gabriel is complete.

It is only as a result of some such analysis that the organization and structure of "The Dead" can be seen to be not only effective but inevitable. It is a story which, in the elaborateness of its technique and variations of its prose style (the cadenced inversions of the final passage form a deliberate contrast with the style of the earlier descriptions, adding their share to the presentation of the main theme), stands apart from the others in *Dubliners*. Joyce's versatility is already apparent. "Ivy Day in the Committee Room" has the texture of a Katherine Mansfield story but with a firmness of outline and presentation that Katherine Mansfield lacked in all but two or three of her works. "The Dead" is in a more traditional style, but done with a subtlety and a virtuosity that makes it one of the most remarkable short stories of the present century.

"The Dead" was not part of the original draft of *Dubliners*. It was added later, at a time when Joyce was becoming increasingly preoccupied with the problem of aesthetics. The story is, indeed, a symbolic statement of the aesthetic attitude that he came to accept. Gabriel moves from an egocentric to an impersonal point of view just as the artist (according to

Joyce's explanation in *A Portrait of the Artist as a Young Man*) moves from the personal lyrical method to the impersonal dramatic approach. The indifferent acceptance of life as something revolving not round the artist's ego but on its independent axis is for Joyce the ideal aesthetic attitude. Thus "The Dead" is, in some sense, a fable illustrating Joyce's view of the nature of the artist's attitude. It reflects his preoccupation with the problem of defining the aesthetic point of view at this period.

5

"*Ulysses*" and "*Finnegans Wake*" The Aesthetic Problem

Joyce's second prose work of importance, *A Portrait of the Artist as a Young Man*, can be judged on three levels: as a personal catharsis, as autobiography, and as art. The literary critic is not necessarily interested in forming any judgment on the first level, but he must take both the second two into account if an adequate literary estimate of the work is to be made. As indicated by the title, Stephen Dedalus, in all essentials, is James Joyce, and the *Portrait* is an autobiographical study as well as a piece of prose fiction. It is fiction in the sense that the selection and arrangement of the incidents produce an artistically patterned work, a totality in which there is nothing superfluous, in which every detail is artistically as well as biographically relevant. Joyce, in fact, has given us one of the few examples in English literature of autobiography successfully employed as a mode of fiction. As autobiography, the work has an almost terrifying honesty; as fiction, it has unity, consistency, probability, and all the other aesthetic qualities we look for in a work of art. Using the facts of his own life as material, memory as the principle of selection, and his own acute aesthetic sense as a guide to organization and arrangement, Joyce has found a way of fusing the Aristotelian categories of possible and probable.[1] Thematic unity is provided by the single direction in which all the incidents move—the direction toward the hero's final rejection of his environment. Stephen is at once the product of his environment and its critic. The culmination in self-imposed exile is much more than a casual decision: it is both an important crisis in Stephen's (Joyce's) life and the inevitable conclusion of a work of art. The skill Joyce shows in consistently painting Stephen's environment as seen through the eyes of Stephen at the age he was at the time, instead of painting in a background which, though valid in itself, would be out of perspective as part of the portrait, shows his main purpose to have been to depict the development of Stephen's relation to the Ireland that made him, from being a part of that world, rolled round with it unresisting and uncomprehending, to becoming a conscious and separate unit able to move in another direction. Such a purpose, and such a method of carrying out that purpose, makes for greater truth in autobiography as well as greater effectiveness in fiction.

In *A Portrait of the Artist*, Stephen expresses his determination "to discover the mode of life or of art whereby his spirit could express itself in unfettered freedom." This insistence on "unfettered freedom" led Joyce to feel that actual physical exile was necessary before he could look back on Dublin with

---

[1] The degree to which Joyce altered, selected, compressed, and in general repatterned the actual facts of his autobiography can be seen in the difference between the long fragment of the original version (published posthumously as *Stephen Hero*) and the finished *Portrait*.

the supreme objectivity which could enable him to present life there as a microcosm of all human history. His exile was part of his aesthetic. In Joyce the traditional bohemian rejection of middle-class respectability combined with his sense of the inadequacy of the environment in which he grew up to reinforce the critical position he first developed during his student days, that the true literary artist, "like the God of creation, remains within or behind or beyond or above his handiwork, invisible, refined out of existence, indifferent, paring his finger nails." Only by remaining thus aloof can he achieve that comedy of multiple identification, that simultaneous taking of all points of view, which is Joyce's way of solving the problem of selection and significance. The "alienation of the artist" is a commonplace of twentieth-century thought; for Joyce that alienation was both a personal need and a creative necessity. All life was contained in Dublin, but to see Dublin as containing all life, to see Leopold Bloom as simultaneously the hero of the *Odyssey* and the shabby Irish-Jewish advertisement canvasser, to see the various Dublin characters while they went about their business on June 16, 1904, as weaving a pattern which projected everything both noble and fatuous which men are capable of, Joyce had to be absolutely uncommitted, taking no sides, free to render all points of view. On Joyce's view of literary art the artist must be an exile, and *The Portrait of an Artist* is a cunning patterning of elements from his own childhood and youth so as to show how for a potential artist to grow up is to move steadily toward the recognition of the necessity of exile.

Joyce calls his hero Stephen Dedalus, and prefixes the *Portrait* with a line from Ovid describing how in Greek mythology Daedalus, the "fabulous artificer" who made the famous labyrinth in Crete, turned to new and unknown skills. "*Et ignotas animum dimittit in artes*"—"And he set his mind to unknown arts." The original Daedalus, having made the labyrinth, was himself imprisoned in it by the tyrant Minos, from whom he escaped over the sea by making himself artificial wings. Society makes its tyrannical claims on the artist, but the true artist can fashion himself wings with which to escape. In both the *Portrait* and *Ulysses* Stephen sees the sea gulls flying over Dublin as symbols of the artist's flight, encouraging him to fly into exile and there re-create the world with the word:

> Now, at the name of the fabulous artificer, he seemed to hear the noise of dim waves and to see a winged form flying above the waves and slowly climbing the air. What did it mean? Was it a quaint device opening the page of some mediaeval book of prophecies and symbols, a hawklike man flying sunward above the sea, a prophecy of the end he had been born to serve and had been following through the mists of childhood and boyhood, a symbol of the artist forging anew in his workshop out of the sluggish matter of the earth a new soaring impalpable imperishable being?

This passage occurs toward the end of the *Portrait* and represents Stephen's inward response to the banter of his fellow students. He receives no real understanding from his fellows, and that, too, is part of the artist's destiny. If his last name of Dedalus symbolizes his relationship to the first Greek artificer, Daedalus, so his first name, that of the first Christian martyr, symbolizes the artist's relation to a necessarily hostile society. The artist is at the same time exile, hero, and martyr.

A Portrait of the Artist is organized with supreme skill to show the movement toward self-realization as artist and acceptance of the necessity of exile as coterminous. There is nothing in the book that is not in some way relevant to this theme, so that the book is precisely what its title says, a portrait of the artist as a young man. It opens with the infant Stephen listening to a story being told him by his father—the child's interest in narrative art is the first fact about him we learn—then we see him remembering songs or responding to simple rhymes. The rhythms of the prose change (and it should be noted that the book is told in a most effective variety of prose styles, each convincingly rendering the appropriate mood and situation) when we first see young Stephen at school, responding to sights and sounds with the as yet unrealized eyes and ears of the artist. He notes the noise of the gas light that burns in the school corridor at night, "a light noise like a little song" that is to reappear fraught with multiple meaning in the "Night-town" scene of *Ulysses*. He wallows in self-pity and thinks of sad poems that correspond to his mood, thus exhibiting what we are to learn later is the first and simplest of literary attitudes, the subjective and lyrical. The true artist must move on from the lyrical through the epic to the dramatic, the ultimate artistic mode, the mode of impersonality and microcosmic expansion—and of exile. That comes later: the final section of the book, which takes the form of the transcription of Stephen's diary while he prepares to leave Dublin in order to fulfil his career as artist, is at last in dramatic form.

We are shown the forces at work on him—his family, his country, his religion—and the claims they make on him. The great Christmas dinner scene presents the small boy moved and bewildered by a violent family fight about Parnell, a fight which sums up all the strife and longing and sentimentality and confusion that surrounded the Irish national movement. Young Stephen is the observer—not yet the wholly objective observer, but still the observer—of this shattering scene, and watches with terror and fascination as the guest, Mr. Casey, breaks down and weeps for the lost leader:

> Mr. Casey, freeing his arms from his holders, suddenly bowed his head on his hands with a sob of pain.
> —Poor Parnell! he cried loudly. My dead king!
> He sobbed loudly and bitterly.
> Stephen, raising his terrorstricken face, saw that his father's eyes were full of tears.

At his Catholic boarding school Stephen is made to feel the growing claims on him of religion and nationality, but even here he has his moments of almost artistic calm, when he can withdraw himself into the unobserved observer, watching and listening:

> The fellows were practising long shies and bowling lobs and slow twisters. In the soft grey silence he could hear the bump of the balls: and from here and from there through the quiet air the sound of the cricket bats: pick pack, pock, puck: like drops of water in a fountain falling softly in the brimming bowl.

The rhythm of the last part of this sentence reminds us of the final sentence of "The Dead," and both contain a reminiscence of a favorite poem of Joyce's, the anonymous Elizabethan poem (set by the Elizabethan composer John Dowland) "Weep ye no more, sad fountains":

> Weep ye no more, sad fountains;
> What need you flow so fast?
> Look how the snowy mountains
> Heaven's sun doth gently waste.
> But my sun's heavenly eyes
> View not your weeping,
> That now lies sleeping
> Softly, now softly lies
> Sleeping.

The repetitions and rhythms of this poem haunted Joyce's imagination; he echoes them several times, and always in a context that suggests the first glimmers of the true artist's vision.

But the road to the artist's self-realization is not a straight one. There are moments when the progress toward the artist's objectivity seems to have led to mere cold indifference, to doubts of his own identity and a bitter sense of loss of communion with the world: the repetition of Shelley's "Art thou pale for weariness" with "its alternation of sad human ineffectiveness with vast inhuman cycles of activity" leads Stephen to forget "his own human and ineffectual grieving." The biggest assault is made by religion, and there is a period in late adolescence when Stephen almost imagines himself a potential Jesuit. It has been suggested to him that he might have a vocation to join the Jesuit order, and he is pleased and flattered by the suggestion. It becomes clear at this stage that the career of priest, in a sense also exiled and dedicated, cut off from normal human life, but given the power of the word, is the only alternative to a career as artist. But the temptation passes. "He would never swing the thurible before the tabernacle as priest. His destiny was to be elusive of social or religious orders. . . . He was destined to learn his own wisdom apart from others or to learn the wisdom of others himself wandering among the snares of the world." The climax of the revelation of his destiny as artist comes when, shortly afterward, he leaves his bantering friends to walk alone by the sea and sees, standing in a rivulet in the strand and gazing out to sea, a girl, "alone and still." He looks at her, no longer with desire (he had gone through a phase of sexual promiscuity) nor with the gaze of the potential priest, wishing to influence and save, but with the calm clear eye of the artist. The profane aesthetic joy of the artist in face of his subject suddenly overpowers him: "—Heavenly God! cried Stephen's soul, in an outburst of profane joy."

From now on the rejection of his family, his friends, his country, his religion proceeds apace, as Stephen works out his aesthetic creed of impersonality and exile. "You talk to me," he says to one of his friends, "of nationality, language, religion. I shall try to fly by those nets." Finally he resists the appeal even of his close friend Cranly, and the last words of the book, from Stephen's diary, are an appeal to the old Greek craftsman, his namesake, to stand by him: "Old father, old artificer, stand me now and ever in good stead." He will need Daedalus' help in writing *Ulysses*, that labyrinth of meaning, and even more so in writing *Finnegans Wake*, the most labyrinthine of all his works. It must be remembered that a labyrinth, however complicated, has form: there is a way in, and also (though few can find it) a way out. Most of those who have entered fully into Joyce's labyrinth have stayed there, but that is because of the fascination of its pattern.

A Portrait of the Artist as a Young Man is perhaps the most flawless of all Joyce's work. The welding of form and content, the choice of detail that seems inevitable once it has been made, the brilliant yet unobtrusive style, these and other qualities give the work a wholeness, a unity, and a completeness possessed by hardly a handful of works in our literature. If one may be rash and generalize about national literatures, one might say that the astringent qualities of the *Portrait* are not characteristic of the English literary genius. *Ulysses*, for all its difficulties and its strangeness, is a more English work, seeming to result from a sort of combination of the traditions founded respectively by Swift and Blake.

Yet Joyce is very far from Swift, having none of his personal savagery and interest; nor has he anything of Blake's prophetic and apocalyptic power. Perhaps it is better not to attempt to link Joyce with any tradition in English literature but approach his work from a study of the books themselves. What, then, is *Ulysses?*

Ulysses is the product of a certain transitional period rare in the history of literature, a suspension of faith between the disappearance of one background of public belief and the establishment of another. This fact may account for some of its qualities and explain the work historically, sociologically, or in terms of some other human science. But besides being, generally, a product of its period, *Ulysses* is also, specifically, a particular work of art, and as such it presents for our evaluation what is essentially a new type of literary art, a new type of imitation. Mimesis, imitation in literature, depends for its value on the implied or in some way suggested application of known facts of experience to provide depth, background, even meaning. To illustrate the point quite crudely: Keats's "season of mists and mellow fruitfulness" has value as a line in a poem in virtue of the implied suggestion that the author, and hence the reader, knows what mists and fruitfulness are in experience, knows with what emotions we receive the adjective "mellow"; the author, in fact, is sharing the reader's world, and it is this sharing which makes full appreciation by the reader possible. This is not simply a question of communication: it is a question which concerns the world, ideas or emotions about which, or pictures of which, are being communicated; in other words, the object as much as the means of communication, and the author's attitude to the object. In most works of literature, what the object of communication is in experience—experience as-

sumed by the author to be common to himself and the reader
—is present in the reader's consciousness as he reads, and it
is this fact which gives meaning and implication to the work.
However strange and unfamiliar the experiences described in
the work may be, they are presented as part of a world that
is common to reader and writer: and when this is not so we
have the pure fantasy, fairy tale, myth, types of literature
whose values are different from those of normal literary art
(though we must beware of latter types masquerading as the
former, and vice versa). "A world common to reader and
writer" is perhaps a doubtful and ambiguous expression which
can be misunderstood both through overliteralness and
through undue allegorizing. Perhaps it might be clarified by
the further observation that the world of the artist is never
neutral with respect to either artist or public: the maximum
of artistic objectivity, of calm and analytic observation, will
never alter the fact that the object observed is worth observing only because it is part of our world:

> Whoever you are, it concerns you all
> And human glory.

Ulysses is different. Though, unlike the fairy tale, it deals
carefully and meticulously with the real world, it is yet the
work of a writer who refuses to take advantage of the reader's knowledge of (and therefore emotions about) that world.
No meaning is taken for granted. Instead of adding body and
depth to the work by references to experience, Joyce
achieves this end by writing on a symbolic and even esoteric
level contemporaneously with his writing on the realistic
level, so that *Ulysses* creates, as it moves, a whole system in
itself, outside of which the author never once needs to tres-
pass. True, there is dependence on Homer and other external
sources, but it is dependence of a very special kind—the

Odyssey is simply a clue to Joyce's symbols, and the important fact is that the work should depend for its complete elucidation on the utilization of such keys rather than on the appeal to what the reader knows about life. In other words, Joyce's procedure in *Ulysses*, as in *Finnegans Wake*, does not involve mimesis at all; it is re-creation, not imitation. The use and value of imitation (all imitation, including that of the artist) depends on the relation of the work of imitation to the thing imitated; the former depends on the latter. But Joyce seems to intend his work to have a validity quite independent of our knowledge of the world he presents to us. He re-creates it complete, in all its dimensions, with no attempt to exploit the traditional ties provided by sympathy and recognition.

It might seem pretentious to seek at this stage for a definition of a work of art. But to make our point clear, at least a tentative definition is necessary. In one of its aspects—to go no farther—a work of art is a pattern which has value for us because the world, and our experience of it, exists. (The difficulties of the critics who appraise a work of art as pattern simply *qua* pattern become manifest when they seek to meet the question of the relation of form to content.) Joyce, however, in *Ulysses* seeks to create all his own value as he goes along. He will not use the outside world: he himself creates all that he wishes to use. And that is one reason why this vast work confines itself to the incidents of one day and the experiences in that day of a very limited number of characters. To create your universe as you go along is an exhausting task, and if you are to be successful you must limit very strictly the field of your activity. So *Ulysses* opens at eight o'clock in the morning of June 16, 1904, and closes at two o'clock the following morning.

We have already noticed Joyce's aloofness and have related

it to Stephen's progressive rejection of his environment in the *Portrait of the Artist*. To Joyce, by the time he writes *Ulysses*, the activity of men in the world is an objectively existing phenomenon, like the movements of the planets: there is nowhere any recognition that the author is part of the phenomena he describes, no recognition that the world of *Ulysses* has value for the readers as being their world. The development of the omniscient author to the point at which he assumes knowledge of the very "stream of consciousness" of his characters, and puts into words states of mind which are not articulate even in those who are described as owning them, means also that the author has made a significant retreat from the world he is depicting. You cannot be God and man simultaneously; you cannot assume perfect knowledge of that of which you are yourself a part. Samuel Richardson, in assuming a knowledge of the workings of Pamela's mind, introduced the epistolary device and sheltered behind the familiar objectivity of letters, however improbable the writing of such a quantity of detailed letters may have been. The nineteenth century had a fondness for the hidden (and, of course, subsequently discovered) documentary confession or the lengthy unburdening of the bosom—devices, like Richardson's letters, which are but variations of the classical and highly useful confidant. All these devices show at least a theoretical limitation of the author's omniscience, and not simply from considerations of probability. (The devices are often sufficiently improbable in themselves.) Such limitation of omniscience, however nominal, is an unconscious tribute to the author's desire not to cut himself off from the world in which his characters live but to admit a stake of his own in that world. The growth of the more frankly psychological novel in the latter half of the nineteenth century represents a movement which tended to force the writer, if not completely outside of, at least to some distance away from, the world he imitated. Joyce's *Ulysses* is, in one of its aspects, the culmination of this movement: omniscience and aloofness are now seen in some causal relation. And so again we have a paradoxical relationship between the subjective and the objective, the subjective novel ending up by becoming objective to the point where re-creation replaces imitation. Of course, this is not the complete explanation of Joyce's aloofness, but it is an interesting point of connection between his technique and his attitude.

In some ways Joyce is more terrible than Swift, for Swift at least hated men in the mass, and to hate is to admit some sort of personal relation. But Joyce would no more think of hating Leopold Bloom than he would think of hating a grain of sand or a law of dynamics. To assert that such an attitude makes for bad art is not very helpful; if anything, it makes for too perfect art. Art is—to attempt another definition from another point of view—a state of unstable equilibrium between what is expressed and what is assumed. Joyce endeavors to express everything and to assume nothing; he makes his work terrifyingly complete, and in doing so shows, in spite of himself, the tendency of art to defeat itself. If we consider a sculptor endeavoring to make his work more and more like his model, improving his work with each stroke, and then imagine the final stroke resulting in the model appearing instead of the piece of sculpture, we can understand how—apart from all theories of the nature of ideal imitation—perfection tends to thwart artistic value. Art cannot replace the object of imitation; it has value only if the imitated object exists and the imitation reflects back on it.

To say that *Ulysses* defeats itself would be pedantic as well as meaningless. But it is true that it shows this tendency of art that has just been discussed. The disturbing quality of *Ulysses* comes from its implication that art has an independent value, independent of everything. And this is not so. If we were to relate Joyce's aesthetic attitude to any historical movement, we should have to see it as a direct descendant of the *l'art pour l'art* theories of the late nineteenth century. That such theories may produce valuable art is no proof of their truth. It is scarcely necessary to argue today that, as the moon's light is reflected from the sun, so the values of art exist because of the values of life. Joyce is almost the 100 per cent artist; the phrase, in so far as it means anything, is, indeed, a contradiction in terms, for the artist is such precisely in virtue of his not being 100 per cent anything. Ever increasing approximation, but with a perpetual gap, however infinitesimal, between approximation and realization—continual unstable equilibrium—are the very conditions of his existence.

The view which regards the artist as the professional sensitive man, the naked sensibility, rather than as a genuinely feeling human being among other human beings, may be helpful to us in contemplating certain aspects of art, but it tells us little about its values; it allows us to pass no normative comments. It is Joyce's nakedness of observation and attitude that makes it so difficult for some critics to pass judgment on *Ulysses*. They can acclaim the style, the organization, the complexity, the insight, the ingenuity, and many other separate aspects of the work, but what are they to say of the whole? It is a work that one finds it easier to demonstrate than to appraise. It is a world in itself, and it does not compel us to appeal to anything outside of it. (It is out of some such appeal that criticism is born, however much it may later concern itself only with internal questions.) Stephen had said in the *Portrait* that art should be static and not kinetic. It might be truer to say that art represents a continuous endeavor—always approaching success but never quite reaching it—to make static the kinetic. The static tendency is to make the work self-contained and aloof; but the kinetic appeal to the reader's recognition (not simply "how true!" but an infinite variety of more subtle expressions that involve recognition of the writer's world as the reader's, however indirectly) is the element which makes the work worth considering in the first place. Is there this element in *Ulysses?* There cannot but be, for whatever theories about art Joyce may have had, and acted on, the fact remains that the raw material of the book is the author's observation of men in society, and the author, too, is a man, however he may wish to suppress the fact. The sum of it all is that Joyce has consciously endeavored to remain aloof from his work probably to a greater extent than any other writer in our literature; but that endeavor is, in the nature of things, unsuccessful, and it can be argued that *Ulysses* is all the better as a novel for this lack of success. Joyce is not just an organizing mind coupled with a naked sensibility, for naked sensibility does not exist outside a chameleon. The effect of Joyce's attitude on his technique and on the details of *Ulysses* is worth considering more specifically, and for this we shall take another chapter.

6

"Ulysses"
The Technical Problem

We have already commented on the fact that contemporary literature, all except some very recent products, seems to belong to a transition period between the breakdown of one standard of values and set of public beliefs and the establishment of another, and we have noted that this period of transition coincides with the period of technical experimentation—experimentation not only in the use of language as a medium of expression but also in the selection of material to be presented through that medium. With less assurance about values, with less confidence in the reader's reaction to given symbols, with less opportunity of appealing by implication to norms accepted as a matter of course by writer and reader alike, the author finds, however indirectly, that a greater strain is put on his technique. Technique has to find a way not only of presenting and arranging what is recognizable and, more important, what the reader has already valued in life before he comes to it in literature, but also to present and make convincing, as a world apart, unjudged, unimportant except for the importance the artist can give it by his method of presenting it, a shifting, neutral, arbitrary subject matter with no necessary or dependable emotions attached to it.

It is in terms of this problem that Joyce's relation to his material can best be understood. Having rejected one attitude as inadequate he does not, as some of his contemporaries have done, seek, by various technical and other devices, to make convincing—at least for the occasion that he writes and the reader reads—an individual and, on others' standards, an arbitrary attitude. He seeks the more drastic solution of adopting no attitude. *Ulysses* is self-existent. It is a microcosm of human experience in general which does not seek verification from that experience as it exists objectively among readers—although in the particular case there is, of course, an implied appeal to the reader's recognition—but verifies itself, as it were, by its very completeness and complexity. The author does not adopt an attitude which says, "Look at Leopold Bloom; look at his humanity, his ordinariness, his sensuality, his curiosity; don't you see that this is the *homme moyen sensuel*, don't you recognize yourself and your friends, don't you see the most universal aspects of everyday human nature illustrated?" Joyce makes no such appeal; he says, rather, something like this: "Look at Leopold Bloom as he argues with a drunken Dubliner in a pub; look again and you will see that he is not Leopold Bloom but a heroic figure of mythology wrestling with a giant; look yet again and you will see that he is not heroic at all but ludicrous and fantastic; and look yet once more and you will see that the actual, the heroic, and the ludicrous do not represent separate values, have no permanent meaning, but are simply angles of vision on a single, yet all-embracing, fact: I am showing you all life, to which all adjectives, and therefore no adjectives, are applicable, something which is, that neither appeals nor disgusts, that neither elates nor depresses, that I have no relation to beyond merely observing and that you

have no relation to beyond reading the product of my observation." It is the actual method of presentation which comments thus; it is the technique alone which brings out this
implication; there is not a trace of appeal over the fact and
the technical organization of the fact. The microcosmic aspect
of *Ulysses* derives from the actual style, the disposition of the
parts, the way words are used, the juxtaposition of incidents.
There is no longer a question of a subject *a* expressed through
a technique *x:* there is a causal relation between *a* and *x, a*
being *a* because *x* is *x.* Here indeed we may say *le style c'est
l'homme;* style takes the place of moral attitude, of any
normative view; life is created by the implacable word, and
the attitude of Joyce to his work is that of the word to what
is expressed by its means, the former presenting the latter yet
belonging to a separate category of existence. This is equally
true of *Finnegans Wake.*

"I believe I told you," said Joyce to Frank Budgen (as the
latter records in his *James Joyce and the Making of Ulysses*),
"that my book is a modern Odyssey. Every episode in it
corresponds to an adventure of Ulysses." The reason for his
choice of Ulysses, Joyce had already explained:

> Ulysses is son to Laertes, but he is father to Telemachus,
> husband to Penelope, lover of Calypso, companion in arms of
> the Greek warriors around Troy, and King of Ithaca. He was
> subjected to many trials, but with wisdom and courage came
> through them all. Don't forget that he was a war dodger who
> tried to evade military service by simulating madness. . . .
> But once at the war the conscientious objector became a
> *jusqu'auboutist.* When the others wanted to abandon the
> siege he insisted on staying till Troy should fall. . . . I see
> him from all sides, and therefore he is all-round in the sense
> of your sculptor's figure. But he is a complete man as well—
> a good man. At any rate, that is what I intend that he shall be.

Ulysses, then, is the story of a complete man (and good in
the sense of Aristotle's χρηστός rather than ἀγαθός) in an environment which allows him to be complete. Leopold Bloom
in Dublin is man in the world; the other characters are simply
environment, though Stephen Dedalus is more than just that—
he is the other aspect of man in the world, Bloom's counterpart, so that the complete picture is perfect microcosm. The
complete man is necessarily beyond any value judgments; his
interest lies simply in his completeness and actuality, and
questions of worth are as irrelevant as they would be with
reference to the universe, to the sum of things. Completeness
in a fictional character may be the result of an attitude expressed by the author and assumed by him to have the sympathy of the reader, or it may be obtained simply by technique. The writer might indicate that for him a complete man
is a man with all the virtues, or with so many virtues and so
many vices, or with a certain balance between his different
qualities, or with any given set of attributes. This kind of
completeness is not indifferent to ethics; but Joyce's kind is
obtained solely by technical devices that emphasize the implications of his character in terms of history, mythology,
and other typical activities of the human mind, and is so inclu-
sive as to make judgment and comparison—and judgment involves comparison—impossible. Thus *Ulysses* is written on
three main levels—the actual, the Homeric, and the mystical
—this being a technical device whose purpose is to emphasize
the microcosmic aspect of the story. Bloom and Stephen and
their Dublin environment constitute the particular; they are
expanded into the universal by their being linked, first, to the
story of Ulysses as told by Homer in the *Odyssey*, considered
by Joyce to be the most complete piece of character creation
in literature, and, second, to various mystical motifs (both

occidental and oriental) which represent permanent tendencies in the human mind. The relating of each episode in the book to an organ of the body and to an art as well as to a separate incident in the *Odyssey* is a further means of adding universal implications to the particular, but not, as with the Homeric and the mystical references, implications that exist contemporaneously with the telling of each part of the story, but which emerge only on our contemplating the work as a whole, when the different organs unite to produce the total man and the different arts unite to produce the sum of man's activity. The Homeric and mystical devices secure their effect by adding depth, like the orchestration of a melody; the lesser devices tend to work, on the other hand, through expansion, the richness being not that of a chord, where one instant gives us the whole, but of a spatial and temporal journey, where the whole exists only by virtue of memory and retrospect.

We can therefore understand the parallel between *Ulysses* and the *Odyssey*[1] by seeing it as a means of filling out the actual story as a picture of life by setting going a series of parallels and correspondences, and the overtones produced by such parallels and correspondences, so that an event is not only an event in the life of the man to whom it happens, but is also related to typical events in human history, literature, and mythology. The specific becomes general by means of orchestration—to use a type of analogy that Joyce himself is very fond of—rather than by expanding the surface melody over a further period of time. And this orchestration is a

---

[1] A knowledge of the nature and extent of this parallel is assumed in this discussion. It may be gained from Mr. Stuart Gilbert's painstaking book on *James Joyce's Ulysses*, which, though by no means a critical work, gives—if rather indiscriminately—facts for which the critic is bound to be grateful.

matter of technique—of vocabulary, of style. Let us consider a quotation from the fifth episode, corresponding to the episode of the lotus-eaters in Homer:

> In Westland row he halted before the window of the Belfast and Oriental Tea Company and read the legends of lead-papered packets: choice blend, finest quality, family tea. Rather warm. Tea. Must get some from Tom Kernan. . . . While his eyes read blandly he took off his hat quietly inhaling his hairoil and sent his right hand with slow grace over his brow and hair. Very warm morning. . . . So warm. His right hand once more more slowly went over again: choice blend, made of the finest Ceylon brands. The far east. Lovely spot it must be: the garden of the world, big lazy leaves to float about on, cactuses, flowery meads, snaky lianas they call them. Wonder is it like that. Those Cinghalese lobbing around in the sun, in *dolce far niente*. Not doing a day's turn all day. Sleep six months out of twelve. Too hot to quarrel. Influence of the climate. Lethargy. Flowers of idleness. . . .

Here there is adequate probability and verisimilitude on the naturalistic level; but also, in virtue of the words used and the suggestions which those words carry, there is the lotus-eating implication. Bloom is walking down Westland Row at ten o'clock in the morning, looking idly at a shop window and letting his mind play with the ideas that the word "oriental," in the name "Belfast and Oriental Tea Company," suggests to him. Joyce halts the tempo of the narrative to bring out with some precision certain aspects of Bloom's consciousness at this time; and these aspects are connected, first, with the narcotic lotus-eating theme and, second, with more remote mystical motifs connected with the associations which the lotus has had in oriental thought. These suggestions reflect back on such an otherwise irrelevant incident as Mr. Bloom's inhaling his hair oil and relate that, too, to the other levels in this episode. Or take this, from the Proteus episode:

Their dog ambled about a bank of dwindling sand, trotting, sniffing on all sides. Looking for something lost in a past life. Suddenly he made off like a bounding hare, ears flung back, chasing the shadow of a low-skimming gull. The man's shrieked whistle struck his limp ears. He turned, bounded back, came nearer, trotted on twinkling shanks. On a field tenney a buck, trippant, proper, unattired. At the lacefringe of the tide he halted with stiff forehoofs, seawardpointed ears. His snout lifted barked at the wavenoise, herds of seamorse. They serpented towards his feet, curling, unfurling many crests, every ninth, breaking, plashing, from afar, from farther out, waves and waves.

This description of a dog observed by Stephen on the shore becomes more than just this in virtue of the language through which it is presented. (It would be necessary to quote several pages to illustrate this fully.) Discussing a later paragraph in the same episode, Joyce said to Frank Budgen, "That's all in the Protean character of the thing. Everything changes: land, water, dog, time of day. Parts of speech change, too. [Budgen had exclaimed at 'almosting,' used as a verb.] Adverb becomes verb." The Protean idea of change—related to a profounder view of perception and substance—is introduced through technique, in virtue of the way the words are handled. Perhaps the most obvious of all the examples in *Ulysses* of implication through technique is the "Oxen of the Sun" episode, which takes place in the maternity hospital: here the motifs of birth and embryonic development are suggested by the style, which runs the gamut of English prose style from Anglo-Saxon epic to modern American slang.

Orchestration of this kind is something very unusual in literature. Most writers are content to supply the melody in the confident belief that the reader, out of his own sense of emotional and other values, will supply the harmonies. But this is not the kind of task Joyce leaves to the reader. The reader has, indeed, a task, but it is a task comparable to the scholar's recovery of the text of a classic or the Greek professor's inquiry into the exact shade of meaning a certain word used by Pindar would have had for the Greeks in Pindar's time—it is a preliminary task, not constant co-operation which has to be given all the time the reader reads; a task in which Mr. Gilbert can help us and in which a familiarity with the *Odyssey* can help us. Given this preliminary recovery of the text, there is no further duty expected by Joyce of the reader, apart from reading the book with a passive understanding. He does not call upon the reader to supply the lower notes of chords, to sing a bass to his trebles: he has written a full and self-sufficient score himself. It is a point we have discussed in the previous chapter; here it is only to be noted that, as well as implying an aesthetic theory, this attitude imposes on Joyce's technique a terrific responsibility. In *Ulysses*, as in *Finnegans Wake*, individual becomes microcosm through the means of expression.

In endeavoring to present the microcosmic implications of his theme by means of the style through which the narrative is presented, Joyce has to face a problem in technique that has not confronted many writers of fiction. This is the problem of contemporaneity. The adventures of Bloom simply understood as the adventures of an individual in a given environment can be told effectively in chronological sequence, one thing happening at a time and one thing therefore being narrated at a time. But if Bloom's adventures are part of a pattern which is designed as a microcosm of human experience in general, and if what is happening to other parts of the pattern—e.g., Stephen Dedalus—at the same time must therefore be appreciated at the same time, then Joyce has to

make us aware of that pattern by showing us, contemporaneously, actions which take place in different parts of
Dublin. Stephen rises in the Martello tower, goes with Mulligan and Haines to the beach, and then proceeds to the school
where he is teaching. At the same time Bloom rises in his
home at Eccles Street and carries out different, but in some
symbolic sense parallel, activities. In reading of the actions of
the one we must be aware of those of the other. Simple
alternate narrative is not enough: Joyce must also employ
other devices.

And Joyce does employ other devices. The first three episodes deal with Stephen and his companions; the next three
deal with Bloom; then follows the newspaper-office scene,
where we see something of both; in the following episodes
Stephen and Bloom unconsciously chase each other, sometimes appearing together for a brief moment, until the scene
in the hospital, where they meet, followed by the night town
scene where their association reaches a climax, followed in
turn by the joint journey home, with the concluding episode
devoted to Mrs. Bloom's soliloquy. But there is more to
Joyce's method than mere alternation and juxtaposition of
this kind. In the episodes which deal separately with Stephen
and Bloom innumerable subtle cross-references from one to
the other occur, so that the alert reader is reminded that
while, say, Bloom is walking down Eccles Street, meditating
on some mundane matter, Stephen, at that identical instant,
is sitting on a rock on the beach, meditating on some metaphysical problem. The reference is generally subtle and
tucked away in some unimportant phrase. The cloud casually
observed by Stephen on the beach might be described in almost the same words as Bloom notices it from Eccles Street.
Or an important key word might slide into both their con-

sciousnesses at the same time, although the reader will not come to its second appearance until he comes to the episode dealing with the second consciousness. It might be objected that such a method of indicating contemporaneity is over-subtle: the reader will not notice it unless his memory and observation in reading are both very much above the average, or unless it is pointed out to him by the critic. This is true; yet an answer might be made that *Ulysses* by its very nature is not meant to be fully appreciated at a first reading, and that repeated careful reading will bring out these half-hidden devices even if an almost superhuman alertness is required to appreciate them at the first perusal.

But this device of introducing cross-references from Bloom's consciousness to the contemporaneous but spatially removed consciousness of Stephen is but one of many employed by Joyce to emphasize the relationship of each part of the pattern to the whole. Throughout the opening episodes Bloom and Stephen, who start the day fairly far apart, move closer together, and this seems to suggest to Joyce, as the narrative progresses, more elaborate methods of indicating the contemporaneity of actions that take place in different parts of the city. In the newspaper-office scene, and also in the library scene, Bloom flits in and out of the background of Stephen's environment, and his activity is emphasized by persons in Stephen's group occasionally referring to Bloom in conversation. But, though this device has its purposes, as an indication of the unity of spatially different events it is rather clumsy and unconvincing. A better device for this purpose is that employed in the "wandering rocks" episode, where the reader's attention is directed successively to different characters moving about the streets of Dublin at the same time. Two or three paragraphs about one character or group of characters, and then we are switched over to another character or group moving in a different part of the city at the same time. Here again mere alternation is not enough, and in addition Joyce introduces, without warning, sentences from an earlier or later set of paragraphs which are quite irrelevant to the event being described in this particular spot but which refer to something happening elsewhere at exactly the same time. Thus:

> He stood to read the card in his hand.
>
> "The reverend Hugh C. Love, Rathcoffey. Present address: Saint Michael's, Sallins. Nice young chap he is. He's writing a book about the Fitzgeralds he told me. He's well up in history, faith."
>
> The young woman with slow care detached from her light skirt a clinging twig.
>
> "I though you were at a new gunpowder plot," J. J. O'Molloy said.

Here the conversation between Lambert and O'Molloy is interrupted by a totally irrelevant description of a young woman detaching a twig from her skirt. This young woman we have already seen in the group of paragraphs describing Father Conmee's progress through the Dublin streets and fields. The point of her introduction again, here, is to remind us that the incident previously described took place at exactly the same time as the incident at present being described. And such reminders are necessary because Joyce wishes us to keep constantly in mind the fact that all these diverse things are one—constituting a single pattern, a microcosm of the human world. When we shift from place to place we are reminded of time as the unifying dimension; when we progress in time we are reminded of place as the unifying dimension; and throughout there is the greater, thematic unity suggested by recurring symbols and innumerable other stylistic devices as well as the nature of the story itself.

An interesting device used by Joyce to tie up the different groups in the "wandering rocks" episode is the concluding description of the viceregal procession. The procession passes rapidly through the streets of Dublin, collecting, as it were, the different characters by overtaking them one by one, and we are presented in rapid succession with the reactions to the procession of each individual or group. Thus the unity underlying these diverse elements is again emphasized. (It is to be noted that there are two contradictory tendencies in *Ulysses*, resulting from its being planned as a microcosm; on the one hand, a few characters in a very limited time and space are expanded by innumerable technical devices to imply the sum of human experience; and, on the other, such diversity as there is in characters and in the dimensions through which they are presented is carefully and deliberately resolved into a unity, dimensionally as well as thematically, because the microcosmic aspect of the story forbids equally any impression of the fragmentary, such as is given by disparate units.) The temporal relation between this episode and the following (the "sirens") is indicated by the occurrence toward the end of this episode of the same description of the two barmaids which opens the "sirens." We see them in the "wandering rocks" episode, watching the procession through the window; they are still at the window, with the hoofs of the viceregal horses clattering away into the distance, when we see them in the "sirens."

The events in the "wandering rocks" episode are not, of course, all absolutely contemporaneous. A little under an hour passes altogether. Time is marked by frequent references to the movements of a crumpled throwaway—a re-

vivalist handbill thrown into the river earlier in the day by
Mr. Bloom—on its journey down to the sea with the out-
going tide. Each time we pause to note it, it is farther down
the river, until it finally comes out into the harbor, sailing
"eastward by flanks of ships and trawlers, amid an archi-
pelago of corks, beyond New Wapping street past Benson's
ferry, and by the threemasted schooner *Rosevean* from Bridge-
water with bricks." (It is typical of Joyce's technique that
we have already seen the "Rosevean," though at that time
ignorant of her name, through Stephen's eyes as he looked
out to sea from the beach in the morning, and we are to hear
of her again when, at night, with Bloom and Stephen, we
meet the sailor who was discharged from her that afternoon.)

Joyce's use of the viceregal procession to emphasize contemporaneity and of the crumpled throwaway to mark the
passage of time can be paralleled by many other passages in
Ulysses. The cuckoo clock strikes nine at the conclusion of
the "Nausicaä" episode, and we are switched to a different
scene between each group of three chimes. The use of a
striking clock, with spatially diverse incidents taking place
between the first and the last chime, is perhaps the most
obvious device to indicate that the author is pausing in time
while moving in space. Virginia Woolf's use of clocks in
Mrs. Dalloway is a parallel that suggests itself at once; Big
Ben and Joyce's cuckoo clock serve exactly the same function, though in *Mrs. Dalloway* the clock device is more consistently used than in *Ulysses*, where it is one trick among
many.

In the "sirens" episode, following that of the "wandering
rocks," Joyce grapples with the problem of expressing the
contemporaneity of events separated in space in yet a different way, and this time the nature of the device used reveals

the ultimate insolubility of the problem. He takes a specific musical analogy and organizes themes that run through this episode on the analogy of a Bach fugue. After an introduction made up of combinations of the different subjects that are later introduced, the fugue opens. First subject is followed by second subject, and when all the subjects have been introduced they are combined and counterpointed together. There are different groups of people in and near the Ormond Hotel, and each group constitutes a different subject. The combination of two or more subjects is suggested either by the actual physical convergence of two or more hitherto disparate groups or by Joyce's describing groups which are physically separate in a single—and naturally at first confused-seeming—paragraph. It is this latter device that first arouses our suspicion that the musical analogy is rather a sham. For in music it is possible to present different notes in an instant of time, to have a chord each note of which is heard at precisely the same moment, or to have two melodies going together, progressing with perfect contemporaneity. But this cannot be done with the written word. Words have certain overtones and suggestions in addition to their surface meaning, it is true; but there is only one surface meaning to which the overtones are subordinated. There is no equivalent in the written word to the musical chord where each note is heard with equal loudness yet at exactly the same moment, to produce a totally satisfying effect. Nor is there any literary equivalent of the counterpointing of two independent melodies—there is a literary equivalent of orchestration, in the sense of harmonizing a melody, but not of counterpoint. Thus, in endeavoring to counterpoint different themes, Joyce can only alternate them, and however fast the alternation, it is still alternation, not counterpoint. No

amount of other musical allusions and devices—and the episode is full of them—can hide from us the failure of this
major device. Simultaneity like that of music is impossible,
and Joyce's attempt at it is simply more rapid alternation.
Perhaps the closest Joyce gets to musical counterpoint is
when he alternates his different themes very rapidly and at the
same time makes the character in one group talk about the
characters in the other group—or about characters that are
being discussed simultaneously by the other group—without
either group being aware of the other. But in fact the written
word is ill adapted to the kind of effect here aimed at.

So, we see that in seeking to provide implication through
style Joyce is not always successful. When it is a question of
suggesting one activity while describing another—as in suggesting embryonic development while describing a group of
half-drunken students in conversation—technique is perhaps
adequate to the task, but the absolutely contemporaneous
presentation of different themes as in music is impossible in
literature. Joyce makes many attempts to overcome this
obstacle which is inherent in the very nature of the medium
he employs, but with only approximate success. Perhaps,
however, this approximate success is enough to suggest, if
not actually to produce, the effect he aimed at, and it would
be hypercriticism to complain.

7

"Ulysses" as Comedy
"Finnegans Wake"

We have already suggested that *Ulysses* is comedy in virtue of the implied attitude (or lack of attitude) of the author. This aloofness, involving as it does a complete lack of normative comment, direct or indirect, can be related to many different aspects of Joyce's treatment of his subject. In the first place, the three levels of narrative—the surface level, the Homeric level, and the esoteric level—imply by the very fact that they are different levels of a single narrative, a deliberate equation between the heroic and the everyday, between the profound and the trivial. Joyce takes a heroic story and a number of theological and mystical concepts and uses them as analogues and interpretations of Mr. Bloom's day in Dublin. There is here no satirical contrast between the heroic past and the insignificant present; the two are not contrasted but identified. Ulysses the Greek wanderer is not set against Bloom the modern advertisement canvasser, for Ulysses *is* Bloom: so—to paraphrase Donne—to one neutral thing both heroes fit. Critics who have been concerned to penetrate to all the hidden Homeric and other references and correspondences would do well to remember that these correspondences are all part of the joke. Joyce is being comic, not profound.

If we consider any one of the main motifs running through
Ulysses, this point becomes obvious at once. Take the Hamlet
motif, which reaches its climax in the library scene but which
emerges in almost every episode. This has elaborate rami-
fications throughout the novel: Shakespeare is the ghost in
Hamlet who talks to his (Shakespeare's) transubstantial son,
Hamlet, and his consubstantial son, Hamnet; Shakespeare is
also Ulysses, returning home at the end of his life after having passed through "storms dire";[1] he is also Stephen, who
fled from Dublin to Paris even as Shakespeare had fled from
Stratford to London. Ulysses, plotted against by his wife's
suitors, is Hamlet *père*, betrayed by his brother and his wife;
is Shakespeare, betrayed by his brother and Ann Hathaway
in his absence; is Bloom, whose marital rights are usurped
by Blazes Boylan; is Stephen, whose rights in the Martello
tower are usurped by Mulligan and Haines. Stephen, too, is
Telemachus seeking his father Ulysses, who is Bloom; and
Bloom's consubstantial son Rudy, who had died in infancy,
is Shakespeare's consubstantial child Hamnet, who also died
as a child. This maze of references and counterreferences, of
kaleidoscopically changing identifications and analogies, is
justified by Stephen when he holds forth in the library:

> Maeterlinck says: *If Socrates leave his house today he will find
> the sage seated on his doorstep. If Judas go forth tonight it is to
> Judas his steps will tend.* Every life is many days, day after
> day. We walk through ourselves, meeting robbers, ghosts,
> giants, old men, young men, wives, widows, brothers-in-love.
> But always meeting ourselves. The playwright who wrote
> the folio of this world and wrote it badly (He gave us light

---

[1] See Stephen's explanation in *Ulysses* (Random House ed.), p. 192. The
other correspondences are indicated either directly, in the library scene by
Stephen or one of his interlocutors, or indirectly, in various other episodes.

first and the sun two days later), the lord of things as they are
whom the most Roman of catholics call *dia boia*, hangman god,
is doubtless all in all in all of us, ostler and butcher, and would
be bawd and cuckold too but that in the economy of heaven,
foretold by Hamlet, there are no more marriages, glorified
man, an androgynous angel, being a wife unto himself.

This mystical philosophy of identity is really a theory of
comedy. All is all, and distinctions such as that between the
theological, the historical, the literary, and the actual are
merely differences in method of observation, not differences
in the thing observed. The theory of the Trinity, Shakespeare's relations with his wife and family, the relation between the characters in *Hamlet*, and the relation between the
principal characters in *Ulysses* are all compared and identified.
In Joyce's world such concepts as the sublime and the
ridiculous simply do not exist: they would imply a consciousness of distinctions which nowhere emerges in *Ulysses*.
Qualities in objects become simply modes of observation.

In tragedy we are acutely conscious of differences in value
between one action and another. Hamlet's mental torture is
presented as a more significant thing than a remark of one of
the gravediggers. The very fact that we can have comic relief
in tragedy implies that we are conscious of there being a
world of difference between one type of action and another.
But we do not have tragic relief in comedy. Comedy deliberately depresses everything to a single level—and therein
lies the comedy, in our recognizing as ordinary, as neutral,
what we have hitherto regarded as special or different. Perhaps "depresses" is not a suitable word, because to recognize
depression as the activity involved is to admit that something
that really should be high has now been brought low, which,
of course, is quite foreign to the purpose of the comic writer.

Ulysses is not satire: there is no conscious debunking of the heroic in the vein of either Cervantes or Swift. And there is no comparison between what has been and what is, or between what might be and what is. What goes on is an elaborate and complex process of identification, an unceasing, persistent process whose object is to break down any scale of values with which we may approach the work. This is one reason why it is ridiculous to maintain that any parts of *Ulysses* are either indecent or blasphemous. There is neither decency nor indecency, neither piety nor blasphemy, but simply one vast neutrality. If it were not for Joyce's amazing virtuosity *Ulysses* would be intensely boring, just as Rabelais would be boring without his extraordinary linguistic exuberance.

One of the most interesting episodes, from the point of view of the critic of comedy, is the Cyclops episode, where a nameless Dubliner recounts Bloom's adventure in Barney Kiernan's pub. The technique employed is described by Stuart Gilbert as "gigantism": at intervals the slang matter-of-factness of the narrative is inflated to an extravagantly heroic tale, with the characters assuming gigantic proportions. The hot-tempered Citizen whose ultra-nationalism leads him to pick a quarrel with Bloom becomes in one paragraph "a broad-shouldered deepchested stronglimbed frankeyed redhaired freely freckled shaggy-bearded widemouthed large-nosed longheaded deepvoiced barekneed brawnyhanded hairylegged ruddyfaced, sinewyarmed hero" measuring several ells from shoulder to shoulder, and with other dimensions in proportion. Similarly inflated descriptions occur throughout this episode, until the conclusion where Bloom's escape from the brawling Citizen is described as Elijah ascending to heaven in a chariot of fire. This interpolation of heroic and

fantastic—and sometimes purely ridiculous—description
seems to serve two purposes. The first is simply to emphasize the fact that in *Ulysses* distinctions such as that between
the heroic and the fantastic do not exist; the monstrous, the
mythical, the normal, fade into each other periodically, and
this is part of that general tendency we have discussed. A
second function served by these passages is to prevent the
reader from viewing Bloom as a hero who acquits himself
well under difficult circumstances. It is the one episode in the
novel where Bloom has all the right on his side and his op-
ponent has all the wrong. He has come to the pub on an
errand of mercy—a purely voluntary action arising out of his
good nature (it is concerned with the widow Digman's in-
surance)—and throughout the conversation he adopts a
patient, helpful, altogether laudable attitude. But he is misunderstood and misrepresented. Through a strange coinci-
dence the other characters in the pub imagine that he has
made a large sum of money at the races that very day and
resent his not standing drinks to celebrate winnings which do
not exist outside the imagination of Bantam Lyons and those
to whom he has confided his bogus information. In addition,
his motives are unjustly maligned and he is attacked without
any cause both verbally and physically. Yet he behaves perfectly. He is not a coward, for he has the courage to reply
boldly to the anti-Semitic speech of the Citizen. Yet he is not
arrogant or rash, and prudently retires at the point when his
presence would only lead to further brawling and misad-
venture. The reader cannot but be conscious of the moral
issues involved: Bloom is right and the others are wrong, and
we are in danger of allowing nonaesthetic emotions (as
Joyce would deem them) to influence our appreciation of
this episode. To avoid this danger, Joyce keeps a blustering

wind of ridicule (ridicule from the point of view of those who would be in danger of applying moral judgments and seeing Bloom, morally, as a hero) blowing through the whole episode, leveling down our values, destroying ruthlessly any normative views we may be applying, eliminating all differences between the noble and the preposterous. It is this wind that keeps this part of the story on the level of comedy. Some such device is used wherever the nature of the incidents being recorded might otherwise encourage readers to make judgments about the characters or their actions of the kind that Joyce cannot allow.

Comedy of this type has no hero in the romantic sense, because the presence of such a hero would involve value judgments. Stephen's petty and irritating intransigence is not held up, as it would have been by a typically romantic writer, as commendable defiance of a sordid environment, nor is Bloom's humanitarianism presented with any sympathy. The reader may sense now and again a certain preference for Stephen on Joyce's part, but this Joyce lets slip in spite of himself, Stephen being largely the author at a certain period of his development and the author therefore betraying against his will remnants of a lurking sympathy for him. Even in the *Portrait* Joyce shows Stephen's final decision as inevitable rather than right: indifference is often the product of a rather shabby determinism.

It might be argued that a work which sets out to include, either by representation or by suggestion, all of experience, must be in some sense comic if it is not to be bleakly pessimistic. Hamlet is merely one figure in a busy and populous world, which we are allowed to see intruding as often as is necessary to keep us reminded of that fact; and when Hamlet and the little circle around him meet their death, a representative of the outside world steps in to carry on; the world continues; this was merely an individual who was unsuccessful, but that is no indictment of the sum of things. Similarly, when Oedipus blinds himself in his despair and gives up his throne, there is Creon to succeed, to represent the outside world yielding from its abundance compensation for an individual tragedy. But a work whose scheme includes all that outside world, whose action is a microcosm of human experience in its entirety, can provide no such compensation, and if the outcome is tragic there is no relief, no comfort, only stark despair.

But such an argument is not really relevant to *Ulysses*, which is a comedy of attitude rather than of action. This kind of comedy is not the antithesis of tragedy; it is on a different plane altogether. If there is no despair, there is certainly no note of hope. Critics may comfort themselves by asserting that Joyce "affirms the universe" with an everlasting yea in Molly Bloom's final soliloquy; but just because Joyce's scheme leads him to conclude the work with a monologue symbolic of the forces of animality, sex, and reproduction—the physical basis, as it were, on which rests all that is described earlier in the work—is no reason for identifying Joyce's views with those of Molly. Mr. Gilbert, discussing this final soliloquy, observes that "it is significant for those who see in Mr. Joyce's philosophy nothing beyond a blank pessimism, an evangel of denial, that *Ulysses* ends on a triple paean of affirmation." There is simply no connection between the two parts of Mr. Gilbert's sentence. The triple paean of affirmation is uttered by a certain character with certain symbolic significances. It is amazingly crude criticism to suppose that, in a work so elaborately organized as *Ulysses*, the last sentence of the last speaker represents the author's view

of life! Words like "affirmation" and "denial" are meaningless in discussing Joyce's attitude to his work and any attitude to the world that emerges. Of course, if you think the
world worth describing that is to affirm it in a sense, but this
consideration is irrelevant to Molly's monologue. Miss Ger-
trude Stein has told us that "a rose is a rose is a rose is a rose"
(she arranges it more effectively in a circle); substitute "the
world" for "a rose" and we get Joyce's affirmation of existence—if that is any help to anybody. We look in vain for any
indication of a more critical attitude on Joyce's part.

The "Circe" episode, where daydream and hallucination
are mixed up with reality, allows Joyce to let his two chief
characters indulge in a process—however unconscious and
unwilled—of mental and emotional stocktaking. Bloom's
visions are objectifications of relations between himself, his
desires, and his conscience (if any "self" can be separated
out); Stephen's, in a much more chaotic and fragmentary
manner, serve a similar purpose. But to what end? How can
you take stock without any scheme of values? The whole
process is redundant if expressed in terms of relations and
conflicts and comparisons, because relations and conflicts
and comparisons only get you somewhere if there is a scale
with reference to which they have meaning. Joyce, as we
have seen, deliberately rejects any such scale. And not only
has he no scale of his own; even the society within which
Bloom and Stephen move has none to offer. Bloom moves
about Dublin, and we see his "stream of consciousness" at
work as he moves; we see the same with Stephen; but who
is to judge between them? Where are the social norms which
provide a criterion to distinguish sanity from insanity? The
writer of fiction has two obvious ways of presenting character: direct transcription of thought, and reflection of the

character in the minds and through the comments of other characters who, either by their numerical superiority or in view of some other quality indicated by the author, represent the normal. Joyce does not use the second device at all, for the simple reason that normality is a concept that does not interest him. Bloom, of course, is the normal, average man, in the sense of being complete. But just because he is complete there must be aspects of his character that are abnormal. There is no suggestion given the reader as to which aspects these are.

The "Circe" episode, then, with its dramatic hallucinatory technique, does not fit in with Joyce's main purpose and attitude in *Ulysses:* it brings in conflicts between the distorted and the real which can have no meaning, because Joyce provides us with no means of distinguishing between the distorted and the real, except the simple naturalistic one which will not work on the mental level. This extraordinary stocktaking apparatus does not take stock. There is no conclusion, no evaluation, only a cessation of stocktaking. The truth is, of course, that if Joyce had used in this episode a technique more suited to the essential neutrality of his purpose and attitude, a simple juxtaposition of different desires, moods, levels of feeling, the horrid flatness of his world would have become too apparent. Technique keeps us interested, but it really has much less to say than it makes us think it has. The desperately objective catechism of the "Ithaca" episode is of all the styles the most faithful to Joyce's attitude as revealed by the scope and nature of *Ulysses.*

Yet having said this we are forced by an odd paradox in Joyce's art to say almost the opposite. If Joyce's artistic ideal led him to express and pattern the action in *Ulysses* so that out of a limited number of events in a short period of time he could construct a microcosm of all life and all history, utterly comprehensive and appealing to no attitude or knowledge common to author and reader, the very fact that it was out of his own experience of Dublin in a certain phase of its history that he constructed his complex realistic-symbolic picture of life meant that he could never escape from his own knowledge, from the facts of his own early life. And since the units which he expands by style and structure into the microcosm are taken with meticulous realism from this Dublin life and what he had learned of it in his own stay in the city, there is in spite of the author bound to be an appeal to recognition on the part of the reader. It is not simply that the reader who knows Dublin, especially the Dublin of the early twentieth century, recognizes and appreciates the remarkable skill with which Joyce renders its color and atmosphere and flavor; any reader, whether he knows Dublin or not, is struck by the sheer authenticity of the picture and knows at once that this is a real place in a real period of time presented with compelling accuracy and fulness. For this realistic-symbolic picture *is* realistic as well as symbolic, and symbolic because realistic. *Ulysses* is among other things a brilliant documentary (and this distinguishes it sharply from *Finnegans Wake*, which is not a documentary at all, but a purely verbal structure in which the enormous reverberation of meaning is but reverberation of meaning). We know from Joyce's correspondence how hard he strove to make it an accurate documentary, writing to his aunt to give him the smallest details of what happened in Dublin on June 16, 1904, and to confirm his recollections of the most minute physical aspects of the city. So in fact the best approach to a reading of *Ulysses* is through its documentary character: the reader who comes to the book for the first time would do well to forget all about the symbolic overtones and read the book initially as a splendidly realized evocation of the life of a group of people in their mutual interactions in a particular place and time. The obscurities which such a reader will face are obscurities of pattern which will be resolved if he reads through the book carefully and carries what he has read with him as he goes further into the book. Thus Leopold Bloom's mysterious reaction when he looks into his hat before putting it on to go out and buy a kidney for breakfast ("He peeped inside the leather headband. White slip of paper. Quite safe") is fully explained later in the book when we learn that he keeps a visiting card with the false name of "Henry Flower" tucked into the headband of his hat so that he can present it when calling at the post office for letters he receives from the typist Martha Clifford, with whom he is carrying on a pseudonymous correspondence. If we know *Ulysses* well enough, on the purely surface level of action, so that we can carry it all in our head simultaneously, we shall need no commentators to explain its obscurities. We will still need commentators, however, to direct our attention to the varied ways in which, above and below the level of the realistic action, Joyce weaves his pattern of multiple allusion and simultaneous multi-significance. *Ulysses* can be relished as a rich and persuasive picture of life in a specific community at a specific time, fully recognizable—disturbingly and even hauntingly recognizable—as human life as we know it, fascinating and wonderful not in spite of but *because* it is grounded in ordinariness.

How does Joyce make ordinariness interesting? Partly by his variations of style, which carry each phase of action into the reader's consciousness with extraordinary vividness and

conviction. Partly by those overtones and undertones of
symbolic suggestiveness, that all-pervasive expansion of
meaning, which the reader senses as giving an extra dimension to the narrative even before he has realized that they are
really present. And partly by an affection for his central character which in spite of everything Joyce cannot suppress.
Leopold Bloom is the *homme moyen sensuel*, half-educated,
unsuccessful in love and business, never wholly accepted by
his fellows, haunted by dreams, desires, frustrations, regrets,
as well as by crude lusts and curiosities. As we know, he is
also Ulysses, and in counterpointing his unheroic adventures
to those of the hero of the *Odyssey* Joyce is aiming at that
constantly shifting scale, that deliberate mixing of points of
view and standards of significance, that is such an important
part of his aesthetic method. But he emerges as more than
the modern little man expanding and contracting between
heroism and triviality. Though he is but half-educated, his
constant desire for knowledge, his fumbling but relentless use
of such information as he possesses, in order to find ways of
improving the human lot and making both men and animals
happier, is an aspect of his character we cannot help admiring. When Stephen, who is not a "complete man" but man
as potential artist, standing deliberately outside human communion, sees the sea gulls flying over Dublin he sees them as
symbols of escape and the necessary exile of the artist; when
Bloom sees them, he is moved to wonder whether their cries
do not mean that they are hungry, and he goes into a baker's
shop to buy a banbury cake which he crumbles and feeds to
them. Bloom's daydreams lead time and time again to plans
for what Lord Bacon called "the relief of man's estate," and
indeed he is in his fumbling way the type of the Baconian
scientist who sees the function of knowledge not as the pro-

vision of insight (which is how Stephen must see it) but as the provision to man of control over his environment so as to make the human lot easier. At all points he is the amateur, sentimental, semi-cultured, his favorite literature popular stories of wish-fulfilment, his favorite paintings pictures that tell a story, his favorite plays crude melodramas, his favorite music tuneful operatic airs (his taste is somewhat more sophisticated in music because his wife is a singer, and, further, Joyce needs the operatic themes which he weaves in and out of Bloom's musings to construct a part of his larger pattern). Yet he is not the neutral, infinitely expansible and contractible figure that we would expect from his ostensible function in the story. For all his weaknesses, vulgarities, and dirtinesses, Bloom remains an attractive figure: in the last analysis he does not let human nature down. Not only are we compelled to see ourselves in him, often our most intimate and unrevealed smutty selves, but we also see in him someone who in spite of everything strikes a blow for man.

It seems clear that Joyce did not intend to produce precisely this effect. It emerges from the cumulative strokes with which Bloom's character is built up while Joyce had his eye on something else. This is partly because if you insist that the trivial and the heroic are really the same, depending on how you look at them, there is a net gain for the trivial because, there being much more of the trivial than of the heroic, in the world, any equation of the two will produce an effect of leveling up rather than of leveling down. It is not Bloom who suffers when by Joyce's technique of "gigantism" he is temporarily equated with Ulysses facing the Cyclops: it is Ulysses, not Bloom, who is degraded. And when Bloom's temporary heroism is laughed back again into absurd ordinariness, again there is no lowering, for he is no worse off than he was when he started, but on the other hand a little better off from the light of heroism (however modified by comic exaggeration) which has touched him. This is not, however, the real source of our feeling of admiration for Bloom in spite of everything. When in the "Night-town" scene he is stripped bare of every pretense and his most hidden emotional secrets are exposed to reveal a startling combination of masochism and messianism, we are not shocked that one of our kind should have his emotional life based on such horrors; rather we are impressed that Bloom keeps going in spite of it all. Further, in his desire to emphasize the Everyman in Bloom, Joyce makes him both part of his community and not part of it, both Irish and Jewish, thus emphasizing the element of exile and the inevitability of loneliness in the life of all men. Of course not only Bloom but *all* men are exiles as well as members of a community in *Ulysses*, as Joyce reveals in many subtle ways; but for Bloom this fact is central. The gestures toward community which Bloom is constantly making—culminating in his paternal attitude to the unresponsive Stephen—are nearly always rebuffed. Now this does not simply result in Bloom's emerging as a figure symbolic of the problem of loneliness and love which we have already seen to be so important in the modern novel. It also gives him a certain dignity. There is indeed a moment in the novel when Bloom almost appears as the "suffering servant" of the Old Testament and the Christ of the New, and it is very difficult to see this role as subsumed in his general character of Everyman. Dignity ought to be merely one of the varying phases in which we find Bloom, the dignified and the undignified being aspects of the same thing, depending on the viewpoint of the observer. But it does not work out quite like this. Bloom's loneliness, instead of emphasizing his representative capacity, gives him a special character, and one that claims our sympathy and even admiration.

If you re-create the world, you provide it with its own laws, while if you imitate it, you have to show it operating by the laws on which you know it is in fact governed. We suggested earlier that *Ulysses* is re-creation rather than imitation, with the author drawing on no a priori agreement about significance or anything else between himself and his readers. This aspect of the novel can be linked with Joyce's aesthetic ideal of total objectivity and his association of artist and exile. But there is another aspect, which emerges in spite of the author. Our human knowledge and feelings *are* involved, and the result is that there emerges from the book a pattern of meaning rather different from that which Joyce explained to Frank Budgen. This is not only the story of Ulysses, the complete man, exhibiting a dazzling series of mutiple identities, demonstrating that "all is all" and meaning is a matter of point of view. Nor is it only a brilliantly patterned paradigm of human fate with Dublin life and characters used simply as the most convenient algebraic symbols. It is also the story of Leopold and Molly Bloom, of Stephen Dedalus, and, in lesser degree, of the many characters with whom they come into contact throughout the day of the novel. And this story is satisfying and moving as a human story— satisfying and moving because of values that emerge in the telling in spite of the author's determination not to commit himself to any values. *Ulysses* is thus an even more multifaceted novel than the novel Joyce thought he was writing. It is both Joyce's intended novel and its anti-novel, both the comedy of Ulysses-Bloom-Christ-Everyman and his symbolic relations with Stephen-Telemachus-Hamlet-Artist and

the tragicomedy of a lonely Dublin businessman, both a time-
less epitome of man's fate and a period piece; both *Ulysses*, the
story of a complete man, and—shall we say?—*Bloom*, the
story of a man who was all too humanly incomplete.

And what is to be said of *Finnegans Wake*, that piece of incredible virtuosity in which the self-thwarting tendency of
art is illustrated to a degree unprecedented in literature? It is
a work that is difficult to criticize as a whole, because it is
almost impossible to read through continuously. But its general nature and purpose are clear. It is Joyce's fourth and
final picture of Ireland. From the point of view of subject
and attitude, Joyce has not altered; he is still marking time
on the spot where we left him at the end of the *Portrait of the
Artist*. The change is in technique. He has approached yet
nearer to his conception of the perfect work of art—the work
which says all things at once so that the life he describes is
all life and the words in which he expresses himself convey no
point of view because they convey all points of view. The
very title *Finnegans Wake* seems to imply that Finnegan, i.e.,
every Irishman, is dead, and activity in Ireland now is but
Finnegan's wake. This is the point that Joyce had made at
the end of the *Portrait*; Ireland for him was dead, was something infinitely other; he had to escape from it and re-create
it from a distance. He had re-created it in the Dublin of
Ulysses, and he does so again in the Dublin of *Finnegans
Wake*. It is a picture of Dublin life—or death; Joyce's aloof
inclusiveness is by now such that he recognizes them as the
same—done by expanding every aspect of it to include every
other aspect. The snow that with its white neutrality had
leveled all Ireland at the end of Joyce's short story "The
Dead" is succeeded by the kaleidoscopic word, which serves
the same function. Dublin, Ireland, the life-death of Irish-

men, Finnegan's wake: that is what Joyce wants to create in
language, and solely in language: not as a man, still less as an
Irishman, but simply as the aloof artificer who has no prefer-
ences, no emotions, no comment; simply the cold lens which
sees everything at once.

We have discussed Joyce's attempt to see Dublin life as
microcosm in *Ulysses:* this attempt goes even farther in
Finnegans Wake. In *Ulysses* the identity of one thing with another was indicated by the different levels on which the
story was simultaneously told. In *Finnegans Wake* Joyce employs different levels not only within the narrative as a whole
but within each word. Joyce endeavors to use words like
musical chords, saying several things at once in one instant,
with no one meaning subordinated to any other. Completely
discarding chronology, sequence in time, as a means of
expression, he seeks to replace it by a more instantaneous
method, substituting for a running melody a series of staccato
chords—yet not entirely giving up the running melody, for
the staccato chords themselves occur in time, and themselves
constitute units in a sequence. If Joyce could coin one
kaleidoscopic word with an infinite series of meanings, a
word saying everything in one instant yet leaving its in-
finity of meanings reverberating and mingling in the mind, he
would have reached his ideal. *Finnegans Wake,* for all its six
hundred pages, is meant to be thought of as an instantaneous
whole; the fact that the words follow each other and do not
all exist in the same place at once is due, we feel, to the
exigencies of the dimensions, to the inexorable laws of
existence, which even Joyce cannot defeat. And so the book
thwarts its own end, for a language so multiple, so con-
densed and telescoped, cannot be read except very slowly,
and no reader can attain the point where all the words fuse

into a single unity in his mind. The all-but-complete microcosm is almost impossible to distinguish from chaos. And the
nearer to completion the more like chaos, until the ultimate
simultaneity in expression is reached, which is itself a contradiction in terms, for verbal expression differs from what is
expressed just in not possessing that simultaneity of existence. Joyce, in his striving after aloofness, neutrality, and
lack of attitude, has sought in pure art an ideal which is itself
a hopeless paradox. A study of his development could be
made into an illuminating introduction to aesthetics.

Stephen's remark in the library scene in *Ulysses*, which
we have already quoted, gives the key to this later work
also. We can compare with it such a passage as this from
Finnegans Wake:

> (Stoop) if you are abcedminded, to this claybook, what
> curios of signs (please stoop), in this allaphbed! Can you rede
> (since We and Thou had it out already) its world? It is the
> same told of all. Many. Miscegenations on misgenations.
> Tieckle. They lived and laughed and loved end left. Forsin.
> Thy thingdome is given to the Meades and Porsons. The
> meandertale, aloss and again, of our old Heidenburgh in the
> days when Head-in-Clouds walked the earth. . . .

Here the puns and deliberate confusions and multiple references serve to destroy identity, to enlarge each particular
into a universal, to break down differences and distinctions
until all things are leveled down to one colossal objectivity
concerning which no emotions (because all emotions) are
relevant. The passage on the museum in chapter i, in which
all the events of history are deliberately mixed up with each
other, is another example of the same process at work:

> . . . This is Rooshious balls. This is a ttrinch. This is
> mistletropes. This is Canon Futter with his popynose. After
> his hundred days' indulgence. This is the blessed. Tarra's

widdars! This is jinnies in the bonny bawn blooches. This is
lipoleums in the rowdy howses. This is the Willingdone, by
the splinters of Cork, order fire. Tonnerre! (Bullsear! Play!)
This is camelry, this is floodens, this is the solphereens in
action, this is their mobbily, this is panickburns. Almeidagad!
Arthiz too loose! This is Willingdone cry. Brum! Brum!
Cumbrum! This is jinnies cry. Underwetter! Goat strip
Finnlambs! . . .

This seeming horseplay, these fantastic puns and in-
genious confusions, do not spring from mere high spirits, but
from a theory of art and its function. This is the human
scene as described by one who has abandoned all standards
of significance.

We have seen in an earlier chapter how Joyce in *Dubliners*
managed to suggest the joint part played by drink and politics,
and by drink and religion, in Irish life. In "Ivy Day in the
Committee Room" the punctuation of the political discussion by the "pop" of the beer bottles, and in "Grace" the
juxtaposition of the name of a pub and a phrase about religion, served to indicate these aspects of Irish life. At that
time Joyce was still using the traditional medium, though in a
highly individual way. An illustration of the distance he has
gone in technique from *Dubliners* to *Finnegans Wake* lies in
the way he makes similar points in the latter book. Here he
does not use the extended method of description in chronological sequence to suggest the mixture of piety over the
dead and drunken joviality that is one of the distinguishing
characteristics of a wake. He uses one word, "Guenesis,"
combining "Genesis" and "Guiness," the Bible and drink.
This is one of the simpler examples.

A wake is not the same as a funeral: it is the kind of cele-
bration where grief for the dead and joy for the living are
equally mingled, where mourning and festivity go hand in

hand, where the virtues of the man who is gone and of the whiskey that is present are both remembered. Finnegan is every Irishman, and, as in *Ulysses*, Ireland is the world in little. The title *Finnegans Wake*, therefore, is apposite: Everyman's life-death, a symbolic picture of all existence. Finnegan (who is as much an idea as a character) has replaced Bloom, for Bloom, in spite of his many-sidedness and symbolic aspects, was essentially an individual character; Finnegan is a multiple, all-embracing concept who presides dimly over the book—he is that Irishman, that man, Everyman, whose life-cum-death this fourth description of Dublin activity is intended to epitomize. And the plan of the journey has been succeeded by the equally complex and well-ordered plan of the organized kaleidoscope, each part representing a different facet of Dublin (i.e., human) activity and the whole being told as a dream and in some dreamlike way linked to the idea of the wake—that ceremony where all emotions are fused in one, and grief and joy, piety and drunkenness, become assimilated.

This symbolic background lies behind a surface story—if story it can be called—whose outlines and whose relation to the underlying motifs are much more difficult to establish than those of *Ulysses*. That the narrative represents the dream of a Dubliner of Scandinavian origin whose psychological state is expanded into and identified with representative themes of European history and mythology the reader may be eventually able to gather; but the relation of the different levels of the story to one another, the exact nature of the complex patterning, and the symbolic meaning of most of the incidents remain impossible for the unaided reader to work out, no matter how carefully he reads and re-reads the book. The identity-in-diversity technique is carried to much fur-

ther lengths even than in *Ulysses*. Names fade into one another; figures in the dream who at first seem to represent
members of the dreamer's family re-emerge as figures in
Irish and other mythologies; places, characters, and objects
shift kaleidoscopically before the reader's eyes, so that no
sooner has something been located and identified than it has
become something else. Naturally, the more complicated
the material, the more rigorous the patterning, and the
schemes which govern the disposition of the parts of *Ulysses*
are simple and obvious beside the philosophical, mythological, and Freudian molds—separate, yet identical—into
which the matter of *Finnegans Wake* is poured. In *Ulysses* there
were the three levels of the actual, the symbolic, and the
esoteric; in the later work Joyce adopts Vico's threefold
division of history into the mythological, the heroic, and the
human as one of many guides in constructing the narrative.
The different levels are less separable, however, than they
were in *Ulysses*, and even on the verbal level Joyce makes an
attempt, quite unprecedented in intensity and complexity, to
make each level include the others and each incident in the
narrative reflect all preceding and succeeding incidents.

This conception of a picture of life which is executed in
words which say all things at once to avoid any normative
implications is a staggering one, and though it is by definition incapable of execution, Joyce's attempt in *Finnegans
Wake* is a stupendous achievement. The care and ingenuity
expended on the amazing "portmanteau words," the colossal
puns and multiple references, are almost inconceivable. Behind the work lies a patient laboring for an artistic ideal
which makes Flaubert look like a hack writer in comparison.
But this is not to say that the ideal is either adequate or
realizable. It is inadequate as an ideal because that kind of

passionless inclusiveness is not what men demand of art, and it is unrealizable because art is always in some sort communication, and the nearer Joyce gets to his aim the less adequate as communication his work becomes, so that a perfect work on his standards would be wholly unintelligible and unreadable, and so no work of art. For no work of art can exist without an audience.

Finnegans Wake is the end of a chapter and not the beginning. It is the final form assumed by the cunning artist in response to the breakdown of public standards of value and significance. The movement began in the latter half of the last century and has already long passed its heyday. Joyce, however, is still the young man he shows us at the end of the *Portrait*. He carried away into his voluntary exile a complete and detailed picture of the Dublin that he had rejected as something from which he was utterly aloof, and that has provided him with the subject matter of all he has written since. Since those early Dublin days he has not observed the contemporary scene; he has not looked around him in Europe or taken cognizance of subsequent movements or events. He writes solely from his memory of that rejected Ireland.

That Joyce should have created what is almost a new language in his endeavor to build up verbal chords was only to be expected. It is not, however, a wholly arbitrary or irrational language. It assumes the existence of the English language as it is, and it is with reference to that language that even the most fantastic of Joyce's words are coined. There is a fair amount of this sort of coinage in *Ulysses*, but in *Finnegans Wake* it is employed consistently throughout the work. Words are made up of parts of other words combined, and in addition the new combination suggests a third word, or a series of other words, besides having a meaning of its own. With patience and thought most of the implications can be fathomed, so that a second reading gives something of the real flavor of the passage. Some of the most effective coinages flash their several meanings across instantaneously and are therefore wholly successful.

The trouble with this kind of dealing with language is that it works (up to a point) if you are the only one to do it, if other writers are content to use the language as it is so that a stable medium remains with reference to which your coinages have meaning. "Fadograph" is a good coinage from "fade" and "photograph," but only if the latter two words exist as part of a stable language with a definite meaning. If every writer were to use language that way the existent medium with reference to which the new coinage is effective would disappear, and complete confusion would result. It is a type of virtuosity which must remain rare to be effective. It can also be charged against Joyce that the language on which he draws in coining his words is not even the English language, but includes smatterings of dozens of tongues and obscure terms like the names of the Hebrew months. However, difficulty of this kind is in itself no fault, provided that the end achieved justifies it. It is precisely this point which remains in doubt.

For, when all is said, the fact remains that the complex organization of *Finnegans Wake* cannot be taken in by the ordinary reader, who will be content at most to enjoy the verbal fireworks of isolated passages. There are some passages of great beauty, others rich in wit and humor, others that excite by the sheer brilliance of the verbal coinages; but an appreciation of these is not an appreciation of *Finnegans*

Wake, which is patterned throughout with almost painful elaboration and complexity yet with a pattern that few if any readers will be able to trace out with full understanding and insight.

A full analysis of even the more important themes handled by Joyce in *Finnegans Wake* would take a substantial volume, in particular the enormous symbolic implications (which keep changing and shifting continually) of Earwicker's two sons, Shem and Shaun, introvert and extrovert, man of the word and man of action. Such an analysis can be fascinating to work out and has appealed to some recent critics as a highly civilized pastime. But there is no anti-novel, as there is in *Ulysses;* this re-creation of the world by the word is single-minded, though multiple in its pattern. *Ulysses* has an appeal to the non-specialist reader in virtue of that other aspect of it which we have just discussed. But when the realistic base disappears, as it does in *Finnegans Wake*, the general reader can only appreciate selected passages, for their wit or beauty or verbal fireworks; only the dedicated expert can master the meaning of the whole book. For this is where the retreat of the artist finally ends: language, which began as a tool for expression and communication, for differentiating and sorting out by naming, ends as a tool for deliberately re-associating what was originally separated out in order to give meaning and order to experience. The function of that re-association is to deny the categories of experience, such common notions as that the past differs from the present and the significant from the insignificant. *Finnegans Wake* is the extraordinary end of one of the most extraordinary chapters in the history of aesthetic theory and practice in Europe. It represents verbal craftsmanship taken as far as it is possible to take it. We cannot but admire the craft; but *Ulysses* remains the greater and more memorable work. There is a paradox here, too. "Pure" art defeats itself; absolute perfection is frustrating; *Ulysses* owes something of its appeal and its richness to the gap between intention and perfect execution. Through that gap human life as we know it and as we are moved by it comes flooding in, and we see that the exile is one of us after all.

D. H. Lawrence—I

Art has a tendency to imitate art more than it imitates life, and any form of art which has maintained its position either as entertainment or as accepted pabulum for the educated over a long period of time runs the risk of atrophy through a too conscientious following of the patterns established by the expectations of the audience, which in turn have been formed by a succession of works each shaped on the model of its predecessor. Even in the nineteenth century the greatest novelists, one cannot help feeling, were sometimes inhibited by the form they felt the novel ought to take. The romantic plots which Scott foisted on his finest novels—those dealing with the complex relation between tradition and progress in his native Scotland—represented a concession to an external form which did not correspond at all to the way his fictional imagination worked; George Eliot's great novel *Middlemarch* is twisted at more than one point, and especially in its conclusion, into a shape that is not the true shape of the vision of life that is being presented; Hardy's novels suffer from the constrictions involved in a conception of "the novel" that is not what Hardy's creative powers needed. "The novel" dominates the novelist, and if the contemporary novel-readers were satisfied, the claims of art were not. Jane Austen was lucky: the form she chose was absolutely the right one for her; her imagination and her art functioned perfectly within the limits of the novel form as she found it. But in the first part of the twentieth century writers of original genius were more likely than not to find themselves inhibited by popular expectations about the nature of the novel and to be impelled therefore to run the risk of hostility, misunderstanding, or flat incomprehension in attempting new ways of writing fiction.

A novelist like Joyce, who asserts his intention of extending the conventional meaning attached to the term "novel" by obvious novelty in his way of handling language and organizing plot, is in some ways in less danger of radical misunderstanding than a novelist who appears to be applying the received formula, who gives no obvious visual signs of rebellion and experiment, but who in spite of this superficial conventionality of technique is really producing something wholly new which, if it is to be appreciated for what it is, must be read in a wholly new way. *Ulysses* baffled many people and angered many more; but nobody mistook it for a novel like *The Mill on the Floss*. In this respect D. H. Lawrence was less lucky than Joyce; for his greatest, most original, and most characteristic work could be and often was mistaken for something like *The Mill on the Floss*, even by many of those who professed to admire him. In his mature novels Lawrence was at least as revolutionary as Joyce in the conception of prose fiction which he was acting out, but he was not involved in those problems of time and consciousness which Joyce and Virginia Woolf saw as paramount and which had such an immediately visible effect on those writers' technique. It is therefore less easy to fit Lawrence into any obvious scheme of "the modern novel." He remains, however, a great innovator, one who puts the novel form to genuinely new uses and broke out of the limits imposed on story-telling by two hundred years of prose fiction to confound the categories of critics and discover new ways of presenting a strong individual vision of life through the deployment of incident in narrative.

Though Lawrence began with conventional ideas of what the novel was and ought to be, it was not long before he gave signs of seeing it as capable of doing many more things than those to which it had hitherto been confined. "You can put anything you like in a novel. So why do people *always* go on putting the same thing? Why is the *vol au vent* always chicken!" So wrote Lawrence in 1925, defending in his characteristically breezy and colloquial way his own practice in using the novel for any purpose that appealed to him. For the novel attracted Lawrence as the appropriate literary form for him to use just because he saw it as so undefined, so free, so capable of testing out a vision of life without rigidly limiting oneself to it. "The novel is the highest form of human expression so far attained. Why? Because it is so incapable of the absolute." This remark, from the same essay, must be set beside Lawrence's prophetic utterances and his violent preaching to his generation if we are not to confuse his aims as an artist with his aims as a sage. "In a novel, everything is relative to everything else, if that novel is art at all. There may be didactic bits, but they aren't the novel." One might almost say that for Lawrence the novel represents a tentative acting-out in the imagination of a vision or a series of visions of the true values involved in human relationships. "Tell Arnold Bennett," he once wrote to his literary agent, "that all rules of construction hold good only for novels that are copies of other novels. A book which is not a copy of other books has its own construction, and what he calls faults, he being an old imitator, is what I call characteristics."

Lawrence's characteristic response to the dilemma of modern civilization as he saw it is not to seek ways of bridging the gap between private vision and public belief or to feel the breakdown of public belief as in any way inhibiting, which is what we see in most of the great innovating novelists of his generation. Nor is he a social reformer, seeking a blueprint of a new society within which the values he believed in could flourish. He soon came to feel the deadness of modern industrial civilization, with the mechanizing of personality, the corruption of the will, and the dominance of sterile intellect over the authentic inward passions of men, which he saw as the inevitable accompaniment of modern life. But he has no patience with political or social panaceas. Sometimes he talked as a wild anarchist, asserting that everything must be pulled down or blown up so that a new start might be made. But the vision conveyed by his characteristic novels is not political in any way, even in a destructive anarchist way. He is concerned always with human relationships, with the relation of the self to other selves, with the possibilities of fulfilment of personality, and with exposing all the dead formulas—about romantic love, about friendship, about marriage, about the good life—which can cause so much deadness or frustration or distortion in the life of the individual. There is nearly always a strong autobiographical element in his novels; he never attempts, as Joyce does (and Joyce uses autobiography too but in a wholly different way), to construct a self-contained world outside himself and his readers with its own structure and its own *livableness*. He projects his novels from the very center of his own passionate experience so that they act out, sometimes tentatively, sometimes fiercely, sometimes desperately, his own deepest insights and forms of awareness, and the lyric and the dramatic modes interpenetrate each other.

If we say that Lawrence turned to the novel for its freedom and tentativeness, and if we contrast that freedom and that tentativeness with the violent self-assurance of his prophetic utterances, this does not mean that his activities as fictional artist and as prophet never get in each other's way. But this can be said: Lawrence is nearly always able to embody his vision of life in adequate artistic form when that vision is fully realized in his own mind and imagination; the murky symbolism, the hysterical tone, the bogus primitivism, and all the other elements in the novels that distress even admiring readers, arise from his own doubts of his own position. One can almost say that Lawrence protests too much when he has some deep inward uncertainty or confusion about what he really wants to say. And since, if he gave himself sufficient room to maneuver, he was always liable to move over into areas where he had this inward uncertainty or confusion, there is not a single one of his longer novels which is not flawed somewhere. His most perfect work is found among his short stories, where he can often embody a personally discovered truth about human relationships in a story superbly molded to embody precisely that truth with a combination of precision and power, of delicacy and urgency.

Lawrence was impelled always by his own relentless vision, which would not leave him alone and which would not let him leave other people alone. Son of a Midland miner and a genteel mother who fought all her married life to carry her children out of the working class, he saw life early in terms of a dialectic of coarseness and refinement which became progressively modified until it no longer implied the simple moral pattern he had first seen in it but a tortured paradigm of the psychological ills of modern civilization, which pushed vitality into insensitive brutality and intelligence into mechanical gentility. Even in *Sons and Lovers*, his first really successful novel (in the critical, not the commercial, sense), the division between the coarse, belligerently working-class father and the refined ambitious gentility of the mother is not a division between good and bad; though Lawrence thought at the time that he was lauding his mother and damning his father and though he later recanted and confessed that he had done his father a most grave injustice in not recognizing his genuine vitality and wholeness of personality, the fact is that any sensitive reader of the novel can see at once that the mother, for all the passionate and moving intimacy with which she is presented, stands in the long run for death, and the father, insofar as he is allowed to play any part real in the novel, stands in his own rather shabby way for life on such terms as life was available in a Midland mining village of that era. Against this pattern of vitality and gentility, with all the qualifications and modifications implied in the fact that the vitality was often mindless and brutal and the gentility often intelligent and sensitive, Lawrence sets the theme of the demanding mother who, having given up the prospect of achieving a true emotional life with her husband, turns to her sons and captures their manhood in her possessive love. With the death of the eldest son (a death for which, in some oblique but powerfully symbolic way, the loving mother is responsible), the younger son becomes the sole target of this compelling mother-love, and he responds with equal passion. The delicacy, tenderness, and sheer overwhelming sense of reality with which Lawrence presents the unfolding relationship of this mother and son make us lose any sense of moral judgment in pure implication in the action. The situation is, of course, autobiographical: in this aspect of the novel, at least, Lawrence was telling the story of his own relations with his mother and father. It is autobiographical in other elements too; the setting, presented with a most powerful sense of atmosphere and of physical detail, of the rhythm of work and life in a miner's cottage, of the relation between the industrial and the agricultural aspects of the landscape, helps to present the very quality and reality of living in that place at that time and in doing so makes implied comments on the state of early twentieth-century England as well as on the relation between an industrial future and an agricultural past. Much of Lawrence's fiercest and deepest feelings in childhood went into *Sons and Lovers:* nostalgia is one of its many elements. Yet it is nevertheless fiction, not autobiography, as we could have told even if the real character who appears in the novel as Miriam had not later written a book to point out the differences between her relationship with Lawrence in fact and Miriam's relationship with Paul Morel in the novel. Paul is in love with Miriam, the daughter of a neighboring farmer, and Miriam loves him; but the mother's love effectively prevents Paul from achieving any adequate response to Miriam's love or any adequate embodiment of his own love for Miriam: Paul is led to seek satisfaction for his sexual appetite in more casual ways, which his mother tolerates because they do not threaten his status as *her* lover. The mother-son relationship thus forces the son to (in Lawrence's own summary of the plot) "go for passion" in his relations with other women, to attempt nothing more than short-lived passionate sexual affairs. But this is unsatisfactory to all concerned—to Paul, to Miriam, to the girl on whom Paul vents his passion, to the mother—and in the end the mother dies of cancer, almost, it seems, an act of despair because she can no longer keep her son as her own unique, pure lover. It is an act of near-despair on both sides, for Paul too is unable to bear the situation and is so wrung by the protracted agonies of his mother's dying that he hastens her death by giving her an overdose of morphia in her milk.

Such a crude summary tells little about the quality of the book, and least of all about the long central scenes between Paul and Miriam where, we cannot help feeling, the fictional imagination is working on autobiographical material in a peculiarly intense way. Insistently, like a drum beat in the background of the novel, runs the question: "What is, what ought to be, what can be, the most vital relation between man and woman?" At some points there is a touching innocence in the way Paul and Miriam behave to each other; there are idyllic moments, when each uses the other as a means of exploring the possibilities of a beckoning future in terms not so much of education and intellectual ambition (though that does loom largely too) as of emotional fulfilment. The moments of tension, of frustration and misunderstanding and failure, are complicated by suggestions of a Lawrentian doctrine which seems to have been applied retroactively to a situation that has its own kind of poignant clarity without it. The touch of muddiness, the intrusive murk, which enters at some point into all Lawrence's greatest novels is not altogether absent here. What is it that happens? Does something deflect the fictional imagination as it seeks the objective correlative of its vision so that it veers momentarily off its true course? Or is it, as we have suggested, doubt, a certain uneasiness about the rightness and wholeness of this part of the action? *Sons and Lovers* is a book about modern civilization as well as about forms and perversions of love.

Indeed, all Lawrence's novels are about modern civilization
(and of course about other things as well). But for Lawrence
problems of civilization must always be focused through
problems of personal relationships, for civilization is judged
by the kinds and qualities of human relationships it makes
possible. It is perhaps an oversimplification but it is not
wholly untrue to say that when Lawrence, in the midst of
handling a situation dealing with personal relations, becomes
too conscious of the fact that he is projecting through this
personal situation some central truth about the nature of modern civilization, he is overcome by his responsibility and
adds a dimension of eloquence or excessive symbolism that
distorts his original vision. There is little enough of this in
Sons and Lovers, which is in any case the most traditional of
Lawrence's important novels, the only one in which he is
content to write the novel more or less in conformity with
the expectations of the intelligent novel-reader of the time.
But it is not merely hindsight that makes us feel that there are
elements in the novel which point outside the conventional
use of the novel altogether. Even the use of physical description—of houses, rooms, fields, farms, landscape, physical objects of all kinds—is different from the use of description as
background and setting in conventional novels of the time:
things have an intensity which makes them vehicles for emotional comment or symbolic counterparts to characters and
actions. And even incidents which in a more conventional
novelist would be used merely to illustrate the kind of life
that is here being presented—a miner's back being washed
(a favorite symbolic incident of Lawrence's), animals in a
barn—have a lyrical passion about them which links them
immediately with the total line of meaning established by the
novel. It was in developing this sort of thing much further

that Lawrence was to make his characteristic contribution
to the novel form.

Sons and Lovers was in a sense an exorcising of a personal
problem which liberated Lawrence to apply his imagination
to other areas of experience. Yet—and this remains a paradox
about Lawrence—though he did go on to explore other
areas of experience and project his imagination with uncanny
conviction into the emotional awareness of imagined characters, mostly women, he could never escape from autobiography and we are always conscious of Lawrence's presence, in one way or another, in his novels. Similar minor
incidents or characters or even bits of dialogue recur in the
novels and short stories, and we come to recognize them as
part of the author's past. And it goes further than this: on
his own relations with Frieda, his German-born wife who
had left her first husband to come to Lawrence, he built his
view of the proper relation between the sexes. This was a
view which was never as clear-cut and definite as critics of
Lawrence have sometimes imagined; Lawrence was continually testing out in his stories new aspects of it and new
modifications of it; but it was certainly rooted in the love-
hate relationship, the endless alternations of bitter quarreling
and loving reconciliation, of anger and affection, that char-
acterized Lawrence's relation with his wife. Lawrence is an
expert in anger; expressions of hate and anger between a
man and a woman who in one way or another love each other
are found in all his novels in remarkable numbers. "He
seethed with fury at the small, ugly-mouthed woman who
had nothing to do with him." "He hated her that she was not
there for him." "Almost he hated her." "Brangwen stirred
in hatred." "How furious that made him." "And dark,
violent hatred of her husband swept up in her." " . . . she

harassed him from his unperturbed pride, till he was mad
with rage, his light brown eyes burned with fury, . . ."
"And immediately his whole soul was crying in a mad,
inchoate hatred against the violation of himself." "Black and
blind with hatred of her he was." "He still remained motionless, seething with inchoate rage, . . ." These passages are
picked out from the first 200 pages of *The Rainbow* and they
represent a small proportion of all such passages in the book
—all dealing with incidents between people who love each
other. The classical passage, and probably the most violent
lover's quarrel in literature, occurs in chapter xxiii of *Women
in Love*. The outbursts of anger and hatred between lovers
in Lawrence's novels have all the same curiously personal
intensity, even though they are often fully realized in their
own terms and convince us of their truth and reality with
respect to the characters involved. But often they seem to
come from outside the story and sweep into it under some
compulsion. The whole crockery-throwing view of love (as
it has been called) which Lawrence and his wife acted out in
their own lives plays too large a part in all the novels; it has
no necessary connection with Lawrence's truest insights
into the relation between men and women and it is also, to
some readers at least, annoying in its own right. It should be
said too that this is no part of Lawrence's criticism of civilization, which is implied in so much of his finest exploration
of what has happened to human relationships in the modern
world; Lawrence is not implying that all this hatred and
anger is forced on lovers by the conditions under which they
have to live. No, hatred and anger are for him on the side of
life, and he can see no valid human relationship which is not
continually breaking out into moments of violent revulsion
as a preparation to further progress in love. Nor is this con-

nected with Lawrence's profound concept of the nature of the "otherness" of the other person, his rooted objection to Whitmanesque merging of personalities and his awareness that real love between the sexes is related to the almost mystical awareness of the essential different reality of the other's self. It *is* related, however, to one aspect of Lawrence's view of love between the sexes—to that modern version of the old Chaucerian debate as to which partner in marriage shall have the "maistrye," a debate in which Lawrence both as man and as novelist was very much involved. Outbursts of anger and hatred between lovers are sometimes (but not of course invariably or even most often) connected with this struggle for domination between the man and the woman, which Lawrence deals with again and again and on which he gives his last word in *The Captain's Doll*. It was clearly a matter which obsessed him personally and in which he was involved in his own married life: the picture of the man demanding obedience and submission from the woman as a prerequisite to his being able properly to love and cherish her, and of the woman demanding a more equal kind of mutual passion which to the man seems humiliating and even disgusting, recurs many times in the novels and short stories. As a counterpart to this we have the kind of situation we find in *The Ladybird*, where the adoring and worshiping husband is gradually revealed as unable to achieve a permanently satisfactory relationship with his wife, who looks instead to the man to whom she can offer her obedience and submission.

All Lawrence's novels are about relationships between people, and his greatness as a novelist depends in the final analysis on the ways in which he was able to project in lively and concrete form his own original and often disturbing insights into the possibilities of love in modern civilization. One does not need to grasp, still less to accept, the full Lawrentian doctrine about life, personality, the relation between the conscious and the unconscious, and so on, in order to understand and appreciate Lawrence's achievement in his novels and stories. In the best of them the full meaning is realized in the pattern and texture of the narrative if only we read it properly and do not look for conventional kinds of plot and character. Yet we are nearly always aware that there *is* a doctrine lying about somewhere behind the story, just as we are often aware that there is a personal problem being worked out. The awareness is generally irritating, for it does not as a rule arise out of the novel itself. This is the price to be paid for Lawrence's kind of genius. The functioning of his artistic imagination in fiction was oddly bound up with the way in which he saw his own problems of adjustment and relationship and also with the diagnosis and doctrine which he felt impelled to apply to modern civilization. In the quarrel chapter in *Women in Love* already referred to, there are moments of the most moving and utterly persuasive rendering of every variation of consciousness in the relation between two lovers, moments which almost overcome the reader by their delicate truth; yet these can be followed by such offensive nonsense as: "She knew there was no leaving him, the darkness held them both and contained them, it was not to be surpassed. Besides she had a full mystic knowledge of his suave loins of darkness, dark-clad and suave, and in this knowledge there was some of the inevitability and the beauty of fate, fate which one asks for, which one accepts in full." Again and again we find that Lawrence will not leave well alone—will not indeed leave perfection alone—and forces a murky symbolism or a hysterical incantation onto the action of the novel to spoil its texture and muffle its meaning. It is intolerable, the reader feels, that such a genius can be capable of such embarrassing superfluities; intolerable that any novelist capable of writing the superb opening chapter of *The Plumed Serpent* should go on to produce such a monstrously overwrought and badly written novel. Has he no awareness of the nature of his own creative gift? we are tempted to ask. He had, of course; yet the very impulse which drove him to creation also drove him time and again to mar his creation with irrelevant excesses. For Lawrence as he confronted modern civilization was driven desperate; he saw too clearly its deficiencies, its terrible mechanizing of personality, its denial of the deeper reaches of emotional experience in favor of a brittle intellectualism, and in his opposition to all this he was sometimes tempted to shout over the voice of the novel he was writing, to shout his diagnosis or his cure or his revulsion or his desperate determination to pursue the very opposite of what civilization stood for. And shouting is not art, any more than that unrealized symbolism he was sometimes led into when he tried to project a line of meaning of which he did not have a clear enough vision to embody it in the actual texture of the narrative.

The Rainbow (1915) and *Women in Love* (1920) followed *Sons and Lovers* (1913) and they show Lawrence moving into a radically new kind of novel. Both novels developed out of an originally conceived single one to be called *The Sisters*, but as Lawrence worked out in narrative terms his vision of marriage, of the relation between the generations, of the impact of modern civilization on human sensibility, of the relation between instinct and intellect and between the rhythms of life imposed from within and those imposed from without —for the novels embody all these themes—he was led to revise his first conception and eventually to produce the two distinct novels. Only in a formal sense is *Women in Love* a sequel to *The Rainbow;* the former follows the latter chronologically and deals with the progress toward (or away from) sexual adjustment of two sisters whose earlier life is dealt with in *The Rainbow;* but each has its own unity and its separate vision. *The Rainbow* begins as though it is going to follow the form of the chronicle novel then coming to be popular throughout Europe, but, as Lawrence warned his publishers, it was designed as something radically different both from *Sons and Lovers* and from the novel as conventionally conceived. Even the opening chapter, with the discursive setting of the family background of the Brangwens that seems in some respects so traditional, gives notice of Lawrence's lyrical feeling for the creative rhythms underlying all genuine experience:

> Their life and interrelations were such; feeling the pulse and body of the soil, that opened to their furrow for the grain, and became smooth and supple after their ploughing, and clung to their feet with a weight that pulled like desire, lying hard and unresponsive when the crops were to be shorn away. The young corn waved and was silken, and the lustre slid along the limbs of the men who saw it. They took the udder of the cows, the cows yielded milk and pulse against the hands of the men, the pulse of the blood of the teats of the cows beat into the pulse of the hands of the men. They mounted their horses, and held life between the grip of their knees, they harnessed their horses at the wagon, and, with hand on the bridle-rings, drew the heaving of the horses after their will.
>
> In autumn the partridges whirred up, birds in flocks blew like spray across the fallow, rooks appeared on the grey, watery heavens, and flew cawing into the water. Then the men sat by the fire in the house where the women moved

about with surety, and the limbs and the body of the men were impregnated with the day, cattle and earth and vegetation and the sky, the men sat by the fire and their brains were inert, as their blood flowed heavy with the accumulation from the living day.

Here Lawrence tries to achieve by incantatory rhythms and by repetitions (the latter very characteristic of his mature style) what later in the novel he often projects more effectively by actions that are at once symbolic and humanly *right*, genuinely imagined. At first sight prose like that just quoted may seem like highfalutin "poetic" prose of a kind we are accustomed to in the Victorian novel. But it is not really that. It is an attempt to prepare the ground for the novel he is going to erect on it, to suggest some of the themes he is going to realize concretely later on, rather than to move the reader into seeing the significance of what has already been narrated. Still, it may seem somewhat excessive, somewhat too high pitched, to some readers. One has the uncomfortable feeling that Lawrence may be about to work himself up to some overwrought utterance not really integral to the novel; but it is in this case an unjustified feeling, for the chapter proceeds to build up the picture of individual and social life in this community, and then to set the Brangwen family into the picture, with spendid conviction. In particular, it gives an account of Tom Brangwen's development as an adult man with a need to marry that is both highly individual, even eccentric, and firmly rooted in what Lawrence makes us see as profoundly understood realities of human nature. Tom's courting of the Polish widow Lydia Lensky— and his choice of a foreigner has something symbolic and almost mystical about it, suggesting the necessity of seeing the other partner in a permanent sex relation as genuinely other—

is presented through a selection of particularities that is persuasive in its appeal to recognition by the reader as confirming all he knows about this aspect of life and at the same time leading him to disturbing and compelling new illumination. The picture of Tom looking through the kitchen window of the vicarage (where Lydia worked) at Lydia and her child is moving in a way that Dickens, say, is never moving, for the emphasis is not (as it would be in Dickens) on the pathos of motherhood or the appealing helplessness of young widows, but on the ineluctable way life works through the complex interactions of sameness and difference between people deeply linked by ties of blood or affection or by the mystery of sex.

It was a brilliant stroke, at once utterly persuasive and powerfully symbolic, to marry this English farmer to a Polish widow, and in the working-out of the relationship between the two, Lawrence displays his characteristic fascination with the tensions and potentialities of marriage. Yet every now and again something breaks out that does not belong to the novel but to Lawrence's personal circumstances and feelings. Because Lawrence himself married a foreign widow who already had children, and bitterly resented his wife's concern for the children she had to leave on leaving her first husband, he always saw the woman as child-bearer as in conflict with the woman as wife. When Lydia is about to bear Tom's child, Tom is presented as hated and hating— temporarily, it is true, but with absolute passion. This is a situation that recurs in Lawrence's novels and each time we feel—at least this reader feels—that the emotion conveyed here is excessive and irrelevant. It recurs in the famous later chapter, "Anna Victrix," when Tom's stepdaughter Anna, now grown up and married and about to have her first child, dances her husband's "nullification" alone and naked, in rhythmic exultation. This incident was regarded as obscene by many of its early readers, and this view of course is nonsense; but—again, to this reader at least—it seems intrusive, forced, and neither literally nor symbolically as true as Lawrence obviously believed it to be. This is not to deny that there is inevitable tension between woman-as-mother and man-as-lover, but to present it in this way seems a distortion of its true nature. Life is not like that, we feel; this is a private bee in the author's bonnet. It buzzes loudest of all in *Aaron's Rod*, in chapter ix, where, obviously speaking for Lawrence, Aaron bursts out: ". . . But then, when a woman has got children, she thinks the world wags only for them and her. Nothing else. The whole world wags for the sake of the children—and their sacred mother. . . . And myself I'm sick of the children stunt. . . . When a woman's got her children, by God, she's a bitch in the manger. You can starve while she sits on hay. It's useful to keep her pups warm."

If we say of this particular obsession of Lawrence's that "life is not like that," Lawrence has his answer. In his last letter to Middleton Murry, he wrote:

> You said in your review of my poems: "this is not life, life is not like that." And you have the same attitude to the real me. Life is not like that—*ergo*, there is no such animal. Hence my "don't care." I am tired of being told there is no such animal, by animals who are merely different.

But this is no real answer to the charge of occasionally imposing on his fiction an intrusive personal symbolism, based on personal experience and not really relevant to the life of the novel, for we concede at once that Lawrence was indeed like that; that is the point of our criticism; he elevates a personal accident to a principle of life. Or rather, to put it more fairly and more accurately, he interprets what is undoubtedly a principle of life in an obsessive personal way.

In the handling of children themselves, Lawrence is brilliant. The account of Tom's relationship with his little stepdaughter Anna is done with moving insight yet wholly unsentimentally, from their first quarrel, where she tries to send away her new father and calls him a "bomakle" only to have herself called in reply a "comakle," to the climax of reconciliation and love when, deprived for the first time of her mother who is about to have another baby, she sobs in distress and anger until Tom at last soothes her by taking her out with him to feed the cows:

> "Nay," he said, "not as bad as that. It's not as bad as that, Anna, my child. Come, what are you crying for so much? Come, stop now, it'll make you sick. I wipe you dry, don't wet your face any more. Don't cry any more wet tears, don't, it's better not to. Don't cry—it's not so bad as all that. Hush now, hush—let it be enough."
>
> His voice was queer and distant and calm. He looked at the child. She was beside herself now. He wanted her to stop, he wanted it all to stop, to become natural.
>
> "Come," he said, rising to turn away, "we'll go an' supperup the beast."
>
> He took a big shawl, folded her round, and went out into the kitchen for the lantern. . . .
>
> It was raining. The child was suddenly still, shocked, finding the rain on her face, the darkness.
>
> "We'll just give the cows their something-to-eat, afore they go to bed," Brangwen was saying to her, holding her close and sure.
>
> There was a trickling of water into the butt, a burst of rain-drops sputtering on to her shawl, and the light of the lantern swinging, flashing on a wet pavement and the base of a wet wall. Otherwise it was black darkness: one breathed darkness.

He opened the doors, upper and lower, and they entered into the high, dry barn, that smelled warm even if it were not warm. . . .

Holding the child on one arm, he set about preparing the food for the cows, filling a pan with chopped hay and brewer's grains and a little meal. The child, all wonder, watched what he did. A new being was created in her for the new conditions. Sometimes, a little spasm, eddying from the bygone storm of sobbing, shook her small body. Her eyes were wide and wondering, pathetic. She was silent, quite still. . . .

The journey had to be performed several times. There was the rhythmic sound of the shovel in the barn, then the man returned walking stiffly between the two weights, the face of the child peered out from the shawl. Then the next time, as he stooped, she freed her arm and put it round his neck, clinging soft and warm, making all easier.

The beasts fed, he dropped the pan and sat down on a box, to arrange the child.

"Will the cows go to sleep now?" she said, catching her breath as she spoke.

"Yes."

"Will they eat all their stuff up first?"

"Yes. Hark at them."

The whole scene, of which this is but an extract, shows Lawrence operating with wonderful assurance and with that combination of persuasive particularization of incident and symbolic handling of objects and atmosphere that he could achieve so well.

In his handling of the ups and downs of Tom's and Lydia's sex relationship, Lawrence is not uniformly successful. His view that in such a relationship each partner ideally sees the other as a door to an aspect of experience utterly new and different and "beyond," and that the combination of affection and desire, of tenderness and physical passion, is not the proper way to such a relationship (as the "common-sense" view might hold), is in the last analysis mystical and incommunicable. If the texture of the narrative cannot suggest it, it certainly cannot be conveyed by such prose as this:

> Their coming together now, after two years of married life, was much more wonderful to them than it had been before. It was the entry into another circle of existence, it was the baptism to another life, it was the complete confirmation. Their feet trod strange ground of knowledge, their footsteps were lit-up with discovery. . . . The new world was discovered, it remained only to be explored.
>
> They had passed through the doorway into the further space, where movement was so big, that it contained bonds and constraints and labours, and still was complete liberty. She was doorway to him, he to her. At last they had thrown open the doors, each to the other, and had stood in the doorways facing each other, whilst the light flooded out from behind on to each of their faces, it was the transfiguration, the glorification, the admission.

Here the doctrine (and perhaps wish-fulfilment?) have taken control, and the voice is the prophet's rather than the novelist's. Nevertheless, the relationship between Tom and Lydia is in general genuinely imagined and genuinely realized, even if this cannot be said for the mystical view of marriage that Lawrence sometimes tries to present through it.

The relationship between Tom and Lydia is soon superseded as the theme of the novel by the relationship between Tom and his stepdaughter Anna, which is carried up to the point of Anna's turning away from him to seek and find another kind of love and marriage. The climax of this phase of the novel comes with Anna's breaking to her parents her intention to marry and the blaze of anger and despair which this produces in Tom:

The next morning Tom Brangwen, inhuman with anger, spoke to Anna.

"What's this about wanting to get married?"

She stood, paling a little, her dark eyes springing to the hostile, startled look of a savage thing that will defend itself, but trembles with sensitiveness.

"I do," she said, out of her unconsciousness.

His anger rose, and he would have liked to break her.

"You do—you do—and what for?" he sneered with contempt. The old, childish agony, the blindness that could recognize nobody, the palpitating antagonism as of a raw, helpless, undefended thing came back on her.

"I do because I do," she cried, in the shrill, hysterical way of her childhood. "*You* are not my father—my father is dead —*you* are not my father."

She was still a stranger. She did not recognize him. The cold blade cut down, deep into Brangwen's soul. It cut him off from her.

"And what if I'm not?" he said.

But he could not bear it. It had been so passionately dear to him, her "Father—Daddie."

It is characteristic of Lawrence that this moment should be presented in terms of the flaring up of "inhuman" anger and even of hatred. Tom's nephew, the man whom Anna is to marry, now meets and reciprocates hate. "His uncle hated him. He hated this youth, who was so inhuman and obstinate." The youth in turn becomes "abstract, purely a fixed will," in his relations with his uncle. Yet we do not feel here, as we do with other scenes of Lawrentian hatred momentarily displacing love, anything forced and uncomfortably autobiographical. The whole developing relationship between Tom and Anna is persuasively worked out to its climax in Tom's half-drunken speech at the wedding which shows him, in his own fumbling way, recognizing the rightness and inevitability of the event. Tom Brangwen is, in his muted and unspectacular way, a true Lawrentian hero, who learns from life what ought to be learned and whose experience, even in moments of deep frustration, is always genuinely lived through.

The novel then moves on to present the relationship between Anna and her husband Will Brangwen. In a series of scenes rendered with passionate conviction, scenes at once realistically detailed and full of those poetic overtones of symbolic suggestion that are now becoming Lawrence's characteristic method, we see the tensions, the love-hate interactions, which for Lawrence were the central part of the marriage relationship. We are shown first the amorous luxury and mutual discovery of the first days of marriage, to be followed suddenly by Anna's turning into the brusque housewife, turning Will out of doors and out of his dream of love:

> And she, with her skirts kilted up, flew round at her work, absorbed.
>
> "Shake the rug then, if you must hang around," she said.
>
> And fretting with resentment, he went to shake the rug. She was blithely unconscious of him. He came back, hanging near to her.
>
> "Can't you do anything?" she said, as if to a child, impatiently. "Can't you do your wood-work?"
>
> "Where shall I do it?" he asked, harsh with pain.
>
> "Anywhere."
>
> How furious that made him.
>
> "Or go for a walk," she continued. "Go down to the Marsh. Don't hang about as if you were only half there."
>
> He winced and hated it. He went away to read. Never had his soul felt so flayed and uncreated.

This incident is finely rendered, and it is only a sketch for a number of increasingly elaborate and often powerful

scenes in which the rhythm of a vital sex relationship is
shown to be based on alternation between attraction and revulsion. Will, with his craftsman's sensibility and his unin-
tellectual interest in the pictorial symbols of religion, is in
many ways in sharp contrast to his wife's female pragmatism,
her literal-mindedness in the face of life, and this contrast is
itself symbolic of a mystical difference between the sexes.
Quarrels blaze up and die down again, and every such scene
has a concreteness of realization that forces the reader to
acquiesce even though he may not be able to acquiesce in the
author's clearly implied view that this is love in action, that
these flares of hate alternating with periods of sexual passion
and satisfaction represent an element in every adequate
marriage. We tire of phrases like "mad with rage," "burned
with fury," "stiff with rage"—"rage," "hate," and "fury"
are words that dominate whole chapters. Marriage for
Lawrence was always a fight. "They glowered at each other,
he with rage in his hands, she with her soul fierce with victory. They were very well matched. They would fight it
out." "So it went on continually, the recurrence of love and
conflict between them. One day it seemed as if everything
was shattered, all life spoiled, ruined, desolate and laid waste.
The next day it was all marvellous again, just marvellous.
One day she thought she would go mad from his very presence, the sound of his drinking was detestable to her. The
next day she loved and rejoiced in the way he crossed the
floor, he was sun, moon and stars in one." Again it must be
emphasized that one does not doubt the reality of all this in
the novel, nor the skill and conviction with which it is
presented; what one doubts is the degree to which it represents the *norm* of an adequate marriage relationship. For
Lawrence clearly it did; for Lawrence the crockery-throwing

view of love was inevitable and true; but we will not be
bullied into conceding its normality, its desirability, its cen-
trality, which is what Lawrence is trying to make us concede. For Lawrence's novels are always about basic human
relationships; he is never content to present case histories of
oddities or exceptions; everything he presents to us is intended to bear directly and centrally on questions of marriage
and friendship and the possibilities of true marriage and true
friendship in modern society. We are always being presented
with norms, directly or by implication, positively or nega-
tively. And because the presentation is so often brilliantly
realized in every detail and also poetically suggestive in its
patterning of image and incident we are made to confront
Lawrence's norms, we cannot avoid them even when we
resent them, even when we feel that here the author's autobiography has violated the story and imposed for a certain
time something violent or eccentric or even hysterical.

The major part of *The Rainbow* deals with the growing-up
of Ursula, daughter of Will and Anna, with her relations
with her father, her attempts to come to terms with her own
feelings and instincts, her experiences as a schoolteacher, her
unsatisfactory but educational explorations of sexual love and
friendship. The whole novel is set in the part of England in
which Lawrence grew up, and places, objects, local customs,
and institutions play their part in this second half of the novel
with increasing power to anchor the emotional life in reality
and at the same time expand and comment on it symbolically.
Many scenes in Ursula's childhood are presented with moving, even disturbing, persuasiveness, and this is more than
the psychological knowingness of the ordinary professional
novelist; there is a penetrating to the real springs of awareness and the very quality and texture of experience. Ursula's

place in the family, her relation to her parents on the one hand
and to her younger brothers and sisters on the other, is defined in a few illuminating incidents (to be found in chapter x,
"The Widening Circle") which not only reveal significant
aspects of the awareness of the growing girl but also project
the family as her environment, showing it as a real community which, for all its stresses and strains, does work as a
community. But if the family works, society at large outside
the family does not, and we are soon made aware of the de-
ficiency of modern English civilization in this respect.
Ursula's experiences in the classroom, deriving clearly from
some of Lawrence's own experiences, are vividly done, combining the kind of documented realism which Arnold Bennett
could have achieved with Lawrence's characteristic use of
the symbolic incident.

Judgments of society are increasingly brought in, often
obliquely through a corruption of personal relations, as in
the story of Ursula's teacher Miss Inger, with whom she has
a quasi-homosexual love affair before rejecting her and seeing
her at last accepting a desperate and corrupt marriage with
Ursula's Uncle Tom. But the main narrative line of the final
part of the novel is projected through the presentation of
Ursula's relations with Anton Skrebensky, a character who
for all his attractiveness is shown from the beginning (and his
profession as a soldier symbolizes this) as too rigid, too
mechanical, too little of a whole personality, ever to be able
to achieve a proper relationship with a woman. His deficiencies are best conveyed when communicated neither
through discursive description nor through an artificial symbolism, but through a poetically symbolic use of action, as in
the fine scene between Ursula and the family in the barge:
Ursula and Anton have been walking by the canal and come

to a barge by whose cabin sits the lean and grimy bargee, smoking and nursing his baby. Ursula establishes contact with the man and his wife, talks to them unaffectedly, receives the man's unspoken admiration of her sex, and clinches the significance of the brief encounter by giving her own name to the as yet unchristened baby, to whom she presents her necklace. Skrebensky remains aloof from this action, dully resentful. The bargee "made her feel the richness of her own life. Skrebensky, somehow, had created a deadness round her, a sterility, as if the world were ashes."

This sort of thing works admirably, but when Lawrence tries to reinforce his meaning by a more self-conscious and arbitrary use of symbolism, the result is not so happy. The moon is used as a symbolic object in a peculiarly portentous manner. The moon rises, Ursula turns to it. "And her breast opened to it, she was cleaved like a transparent jewel to its light. She stood filled with the full moon, offering herself." She withdraws from Skrebensky under the moon's influence, even though he is still holding her hand. She asks him to leave her alone; then they dance together under the moon; "his will was set and straining with all its tension to encompass her and compel her." But the moon works on, demoralizing Anton and changing Ursula. "He was afraid of the great moon-conflagration of the cornstacks rising above him. His heart grew smaller, it began to fuse like a bead. He knew he would die." And eventually Usrula makes "hard and fierce" love to him. "So she held him there, the victim, consumed, annihilated. She had triumphed: he was not any more." We sense that this sort of love-making is all wrong, and we sense too that in some way the moon is symbolic of some important element in the situation. But the symbol does not really work in its context; its meaning has to be reasoned out afterward. So, toward the end, what leads Ursula to break off her engagement to Anton Skrebensky is symbolized by their hard and fierce open-air love-making under the moon. "It lasted till it was agony to his soul, till he succumbed, till he gave way as if dead, and lay with his face buried, partly in her hair, partly in the sand, motionless, as if he would be motionless now for ever, hidden away in the dark, buried, only buried, he only wanted to be buried in the goodly darkness, only that, and no more." Something is wrong with sex at this point, we gather. Ursula lies still after the symbolic killing of Anton by the wrong kind of love-making, and evidently she sees it as a proof of failure and loss: a tear trickles from her eye. They are both crushed and silent. "They were like two dead people who dare not recognize, dare not see each other." Their subsequent conversation is as follows:

"Have you done with me?" he asked at length, lifting his head.
"It isn't me," she said. "You have done with me—we have done with each other. . . ."
"Well, what have I done?" he asked, in a rather querulous voice.
"I don't know," she said, in the same dull, feelingless voice.
"It is finished. It has been a failure."

Careful explicators will be able to point out just why this failure is represented by love-making under the moon and exactly why the moon is used as a recurring symbol in this connection. But this will not justify the use of the symbol in this way in the novel. The failure of love—or the failure of sexual technique which seems to spring from a failure of love —is obviously something important and climactic in the novel, but its method of presentation is murky and overinsistent. The common-sense questions, "What really happens here? What exactly is the matter? Why do they both feel this dead finality afterwards?" will not be stilled. Lawrence's meaning is not properly realized in terms of the novel. *The Rainbow* comes to an end with Ursula's vision of the countryside and its inhabitants, of hills, houses, and colliers, in all their dry corruption, suddenly redeemed by a growing and strengthening rainbow arching across the sky and standing on the earth. She sees the rainbow a sign of "earth's new architecture, the old, brittle corruption of houses and factories swept away, the world built up in a living fabric of Truth, fitting to the over-arching heaven." But the novel has already said more than this, has already proved itself too complex to be concluded by a simple vision of hope such as the rainbow. It is a great but flawed novel, and leaves us with that mixture of enthusiasm and exasperation which is the characteristic effect of this disturbing genius.

Any attempt to come to terms with Lawrence's genius as a novelist must center on *The Rainbow* and *Women in Love*. The latter novel is the story of Ursula and her sister Gudrun and their attempts to find fulfilment in a satisfactory sex relationship. Here even more than in *The Rainbow* Lawrence manages to present some of his most searching criticism of modern English civilization through the projection of character and the interaction of characters. His own foreword to novel is of interest:

> This novel pretends only to be a record of the writer's own desires, aspirations, struggles; in a word, a record of the profoundest experiences of the self. Nothing that comes from the deep, passional soul is bad, or can be bad. So there is no apology to tender, unless to the soul itself, if it should have been belied.

Man struggles with his unborn needs and fulfilment. New unfoldings struggle up in torment in him, as buds struggle forth from the midst of a plant. Any man of real individuality tries to know and to understand what is happening, even in himself, as he goes along. This struggle for verbal consciousness should not be left out in art. It is a very great part of life. It is not superimposition of a theory. It is the passionate struggle into conscious being.

This emphasizes, if emphasis were needed, the degree of personal commitment that we find in all Lawrence's novels. Lawrence combined the artist's ability to project other characters, and see them objectively at the same time as from the inside, with an ability to use the characters as instruments for the exploration and presentation of his own deepest and most personal insights. In a sense this is true of all great novelists, but in Lawrence the nature of the personal involvement seems to be different, as though the novel as it moves is testing out for him urgent yet tentative intuitions which have to be seen projected in novel form before their meaning and validity can be fully known even to the author. "This struggle for verbal consciousness should not be left out in art."

Women in Love is a novel that for the most part brims over with life—with sense of place and of objects, with sense of characters in their relation to place and to each other, with sense of the workings of society which throw up such characters in such places, and above all with the power of projecting all criticism of society and all normative judgments on which that criticism is based through the mutual interactions of people, places, and things. It might seem odd that one should emphasize places and things so much in a novel dealing essentially with people and their relationships, but it is a fact that this novel, for all its fierce concentration on the potentialities (and failures) of human relationships, uses physical environment and physical objects in order to focus these human relationships and builds up, both directly and by implication, a picture of England as well as a pattern of personal loves and conflicts, with the picture and the pattern in some measure depending on each other.

The quartet of characters on whom the novel concentrates—Ursula and Rupert Birkin, Gudrun and Gerald Crich—is not simply a pair of couples: the two men also have a close and testing relationship with each other, while the two sisters are of course shown as sisters with all that that implies. Birkin is partly Lawrence himself, and acts out (as Ursula does too) parts of Lawrence's past as well as something of Lawrence's mystique of human relations. Gerald Crich, son of a Midland colliery owner, is the efficient, managing, modern male, product of what we today would call the managerial revolution and more basically product of the modern world as Lawrence sees it, immensely attractive in his cold blond perfection but in the last analysis unable to rise to the true challenge of love or even of adequate living at any level, and he dies in the end symbolically frozen on the snow-covered Alpine slopes. Rupert Birkin is less of a piece, more volatile, far less physically perfect, almost obsessively concerned with proper human relationships, a darting, feeling, demanding, pulsing, changing human being, who in the end does achieve a satisfactory relationship with Ursula, whom he marries, but only after many characteristically Lawrentian scenes of struggle and doubt and alternating movements of repulsion and attraction in the course of which much of Lawrence's mature view of men and women is given concrete embodiment and symbolization. But the conclusion of the novel, with Gerald dead, Gudrun fascinated by an attractively corrupt German sculptor, and Ursula and Rupert facing each other, is far from embodying a final solution. Rupert demands more than a satisfactory relationship between man and wife, and the novel ends on a question:

> "Did you need Gerald?" she asked one evening.
>
> "Yes," he said.
>
> "Aren't I enough for you?" she asked.
>
> "No," he said. "You are enough for me, as far as a woman is concerned. You are all women to me. But I wanted a man friend, as eternal as you and I are eternal."
>
> "Why aren't I enough?" she said. "You are enough for me. I don't want anybody else but you. Why isn't it the same with you?"
>
> "Having you, I can live all my life without anybody else, any other sheer intimacy. But to make it complete, really happy, I wanted eternal union with a man too: another kind of love," he said.
>
> "I don't believe it," she said. "It's an obstinacy, a theory, a perversity."
>
> "Well—" he said.
>
> "You can't have two kinds of love. Why should you!"
>
> "It seems as if I can't," he said. "Yet I wanted it."
>
> "You can't have it, because it's false, impossible," she said.
>
> "I don't believe that," he answered.

The search for the mystic communion between man and man, *Blutbruderschaft*, is a theme that winds in and out of the novel, and it projects some tense scenes between Rupert and Gerald (notably in chapter xx, "Gladiatorial"). But it remains, at least to this reader, a case of Lawrence thrusting himself into the novel; the treatment is never properly persuasive or illuminating, and one never really knows what the author is getting at. At the same time it must be said that Lawrence is occasionally aware of the intrusiveness of this

theme, and illustrates his awareness by the skeptical response of other characters to Rupert. Lawrence is capable of
laughing at himself, and there are scenes in *Women in Love*
and elsewhere which show the Lawrentian hero being effectively teased and even mocked for his prophetic gestures or
insistent emotional claims. These are not the most memorable scenes in the novel, however. Rupert's conflict with the
possessive Hermione, with her cerebrally willed anti-intel-
lectualism, is finely done in a number of striking scenes, and
there are many incidental character projections—that of
Gerald's mother, for example—and carefully posed events
and situations which help to give the novel its enormous
vitality. The account of Diana Crich's drowning, Gudrun's
relations with the child Winifred (who is brilliantly drawn
by means of some brief dialogue), the disturbingly suggestive scene with the rabbit in chapter xviii, Gerald's forcing of
his mare to stand by the railway crossing as the colliery train
grinds and squeaks by in chapter ix, Ursula and Rupert Birkin buying a chair in the market and presenting it to a half-
sullen, half-responsive couple who are going to get married
because the girl is going to have a baby (a remarkable scene,
in chapter xxvi)—these are some of the strokes by means of
which Lawrence builds up his compelling picture of human
relationships, good, bad, and mixed, working and interrelat-
ing under the pressures of a given society, a society which is
always judged by the opportunities for entering into genuine
relationships which it offers to people. But the often admired scene, in chapter xix, where Birkin throws stones at the
moon's reflection in the water, trying to break it up, is really
less impressive: it is too obviously fictive, too *voulu*. Birkin
shouts: "Cybele—curse her! The accused Syria Dea! Does
one begrudge it her? What else is there—?" while the unseen

Ursula watches incredulously and thinks him mad. It takes no great analytic subtlety to relate the moon symbol here to Birkin's resistance to Ursula's demand for "love" in the conventional romantic sense or to include this interpretation in a much more complex explanation which links up with Ursula's last and fatal love-making with Skrebensky under the moon in *The Rainbow*, but the symbol remains imposed and wilful for all that. And there is also, as we have noted, the overinsistent note of female awe before the male body: "Oh, and the beauty of the subjection of his loins, white and dimly luminous as he climbed over the side of the boat, made her want to die, to die. The beauty of his dim and luminous loins as he climbed into the boat, his back rounded and soft— ah, this was too much for her, too final a vision. She knew it, and it was fatal. The terrible hopelessness of fate, and of beauty, such beauty!"

In view of the fact that Lawrence in his lifetime and even after was attacked with such venom by critics who wilfully and radically misunderstood his novels, it may seem unfair to pay any attention at all to occasional signs of obsession and emotional extravagance in the novels. But if we are to see Lawrence whole, we must see these things as characteristic defects of his undeniably great genius, as intimately bound up with his way of writing novels. A novelist who wrote so profoundly out of his own most deeply committed feelings, whose view of art was absolutely antithetical to the Joycean view of the artist as supremely objective creator "aloof, indifferent, paring his finger-nails," was bound to have faults antithetical to those of Joyce. If the Joycean extreme was to reduce all art to one enormous, echoing pun which presented all possible views of life simultaneously as equally true, the Lawrentian extreme was to reduce all art to the desperately personal vision. A novelist's kind of greatness can be judged by the kind of extremes to which he can be led.

It seems true, too, that some of these disturbing outbursts of Lawrence, nearly always representing the woman's view of the dominating male, derive from what might be called a basic femininity in himself. It is at least significant that nowhere in Lawrence do we get a really passionate and committed view from the inside of a man's excitement at a woman's body, but over and over again (most of all in *Lady Chatterley's Lover*) we get with extraordinary and even overwrought passion a woman's view of her excitement at a man's body. It is Ursula and Lady Chatterley whose experiences really matter, not Birkin and the gamekeeper. The concern with male leadership which dominates *Aaron's Rod*, *Kangaroo*, and *The Plumed Serpent* and which produces his least convincing work may well represent an overcompensation by a sensibility whose deepest characteristics were more feminine than masculine, while the insistent male claim to dominance in love over the obedient female which we find in the two latter of these three novels and in some of the short stories often seems to spring less from a male claim to dominate than from a female wish to be dominated. But such speculations lead us away from the qualities and glories of Lawrence as a novelist. *The Rainbow* and *Women in Love* represent unique achievements in English literature and, flawed at some points though they may be, they have qualities of vitality and penetration and moments of uncanny revelation resulting from a remarkable combination of the precise and the visionary and the rhythmic patterning of events and objects that can evoke nothing but an almost incredulous admiration.

9

D. H. Lawrence—II

Aaron's Rod and *Kangaroo*, published in 1922 and 1923, respectively, have little of the intensity and of the brilliant counterpointing of personal and social fact that we find in *The Rainbow* and *Women in Love*. They are leisurely, half-auto-biographical, half-imaginative recollections and explorations of aspects of experience which interested Lawrence at this time. The motivation is often perfunctory, the relation between the real and the symbolic often inadequately conceived and worked out. *Aaron's Rod* opens with a finely realized scene where the hero, Aaron Sisson, checkweighman at a colliery, is shown with his wife and children at home just before Christmas. There is something wrong with the coziness of the domestic atmosphere, and the behavior of Aaron's two daughters and the dialogue between Aaron and his wife project this with disturbing insistence. But when, in the following chapter, Aaron goes out to buy Christmas-tree candles, drops in at the Royal Oak for a drink and a talk with the landlady, then, when it is time to return home, turns another way "in a delirium of icy fury," we suspect that Aaron is about to be made to play a part that acts out some private obsession of the author rather than develops the lines laid down in the opening chapter, and when in the third chapter we find him stumbling into a sophisticated party at

the home of a colliery owner, and being accepted by the
guests there and invited to spend the night, we are at a loss
to know what kind of probability Lawrence is trying to establish in this novel. The fact is that he does not bother about
levels of probability at all; he imposes an incident from his
own life or from his imaginative fund of symbolic situations
whenever it pleases him to stop and contemplate it, and it is
this deliberate casualness that gives the novel both its special
kind of slackness and its special kind of charm. Aaron leaves
his family in a curiously fatalistic and irresponsible way that
is never explored or explained adequately, and we next find
him in London playing the flute (Aaron's rod) in an or-
chestra, for it suits Lawrence to have this workingman from
a Midland colliery a flautist of fine professional competence.
Of course he makes contact again with the friends he made
at the party, and things happen to him that are very like
things that happened to Lawrence in London. But it does not
take long before we discover that the real Lawrence-figure in
the book is not Aaron but Rawdon Lilly, whom he also meets
in London and whose relations with his wife Tanny are very
Lawrentian. At one point autobiography seems to take complete control, and there is an account of a quarrel between
Jim Bricknell (one of the original party group) and Lilly at
the latter's Hampshire cottage which has nothing at all to do
with the hero and his destiny but which we do know to be a
fairly accurate rendering of an incident in which Lawrence
was concerned. When Tanny (who is Mrs. Lawrence) goes
off to visit her people in Norway, Lilly looks after the sick
Aaron in London—a scene of considerable power and closely
bound up with Lawrence's own experience and his views of
the nature of male friendship. Then, because Lawrence was
in Italy after the war and wanted to bring his characters

after him, he brought Aaron to Italy in Lilly's wake and the latter and more interesting part of the book takes place in Italy.

Parts of the Italian section of *Aaron's Rod* read like a travel book written by an uncannily perceptive and searchingly ironic tourist. Aaron's stay with Sir William and Lady Franks at Novara (in many respects an account of a real stay by Lawrence with a wealthy Englishman at his villa in Turin) is done with both comedy and bitterness, and can be read as a set piece in its own right, as can the account of a political demonstration in the city in the following chapter. Other real characters are introduced and either evoked or satirized or both. But all the time Aaron is bothering about the proper relationship between man and wife and realizing his commitment to his wife as well as the necessity for his keeping away from her (this part of the novel is never properly realized). He plays his flute to an American-born Marchesa in Florence and by so doing lifts some sort of curse from her so as to enable her to sing again. (This is the very stuff of folk tale, the kind of material Lawrence draws on occasionally in his short stories.) He finally catches up with Lilly, who preaches Lawrentian doctrine at him, and after his symbolic flute has been destroyed by a bomb thrown in a café, he goes off with Lilly to be harangued about leadership and the need for him (Aaron) to submit to Lilly. The novel ends with Aaron asking "And whom shall I submit to?" and with Lilly replying "Your soul will tell you."

The curious novel is worth some discussion because in its relaxed, discursive, formless way it brings us near to Lawrence in that interesting stage of his imagination when he was halfway between life and art, as it were. It contains some brilliant scenes and a brilliant rendering of Italy immediately after the First World War, as well as some powerful dialogue directed against the romantic notion of love between the sexes and in favor of something else which is never very clearly defined. The leadership theme is one which is treated here and which engaged Lawrence in his two subsequent novels. The alternation of the travelogue and the symbolic use of incident, and of autobiography and diagnosis, does not make for an adequately shaped novel, and, as we have seen, the levels of probability shift disconcertingly. But *Aaron's Rod* remains full of interest and full of appeal—especially if we are content to read it easily, without researching into the symbolism at each point, for it is not a novel to be taken solemnly, as it too often is.

Much the same can be said of *Kangaroo*, where Lawrence drew on his short stay in Australia to write a novel set wholly in Sydney and the nearby Australian coast. The hero, Somers, and his wife, Harriet, are clearly Lawrence and Frieda, and their perpetual quarrels about "maistrye" in love are by now familiar, though here they have a fierceness that is very compelling and sometimes even despairing. There are three elements in the novel: the relation between Somers and Harriet, the relation of both of them to their Australian environment and neighbors, and Somers' involvement with Kangaroo himself, the leader of a quasi-fascist movement for the regeneration of Australian society. The Australian environment is evoked with remarkable precision and with a half-teasing affection which is unusual with Lawrence and which gives the novel its special air of humane curiosity. Nowhere else does Lawrence show with such sustained brilliance his uncanny ability to distil the essence of a civilization, to get to know it from the inside, as a result of only a brief stay. It is all the more surprising, therefore, that he should have put in the midst of the finely realized Australian society a character and a political situation (the struggle between the Diggers and the Socialists) that was wholly of his own invention. Something of what he saw in Italy must have been operating on his imagination here, and certainly, though the political struggle he describes has nothing to do with the Australia of the time, it was prophetic of much that was to happen in Europe. Somers' personal involvement in this is the least convincing part of the novel, bound up with Lawrence's leadership mystique. But the relationship between Somers and Kangaroo fails, and we feel that this phase of Lawrence's thought has been acted out to the point where it destroys itself.

Aaron's Rod and *Kangaroo* illustrate a curious paradox about Lawrence—a paradox illuminated by F. R. Leavis' quarrel with Middleton Murry over whether Lawrence's primary concern was with "art." Leavis quotes Murry on Lawrence: "To charge him with lack of form, or of any other of the qualities that are supposed to be necessary to art, is to be guilty of irrelevance. Art was not his aim." Against this dictum Leavis cites Lawrence's own words, "Art speech is the only speech," and sees some at least of Lawrence's work as exhibiting "the serenely triumphant reign of intelligence—intelligence that, in creative understanding, transcends the plight that feeds it." Leavis, however, admits that these two novels "were written at great speed in a tentative and self-exploratory spirit, and something like a direct involvement of the author is so evident in them on so large a scale as to give much colour, here, to Middleton Murry's kind of documentary reduction." The situation is not, however, simply that sometimes Lawrence is too directly involved and at other times, in his greatest work, achieves the

serene objectivity of the artist, for his personal involvement
is part of his strength (not a weakness that is dropped in his
best work) and can sometimes produce just that achieved
realization of meaning in terms of art that is normally considered to be the antithesis of this sort of personal involvement. The paradox is that Lawrence's weakness is also his
strength; this fierce personal involvement can produce work
of genuine artistic power. It is not so much a question of his
creative intelligence being able to "transcend the plight that
feeds it," because the plight is not really transcended, it is
used, and it remains visible in all sorts of oblique ways even
when Lawrence is dealing with imagined characters in situations quite different from any in which he himself had been
involved. The uncanny perceptiveness, the sense of how class
operates on personality in England, the feeling for conflicting
rhythms of life (and death) as they throb behind the most
ordinary, the most outwardly drab, situations—these and
other impressive qualities which we find in such a short story
as *Daughters of the Vicar* derive clearly from Lawrence's own
concerns, his own life, his own experience of class and conflict. And if it is objected that of course every novelist draws
on his own experience, embodies his own view of the world,
presents a vision derived from the way life has worked with
him, that this is inevitable and by no means peculiar to
Lawrence, we must still insist that in Lawrence the element
of personal conviction, the suggestion that a given story is
patterned so as to be able to hold something intensely, even
defiantly, felt by the author, is found in Lawrence in a way
that is not found in other great novelists. What could be more
objectively created than the little story *Second Best*, about a
farm girl returning from the city to accept a local man she
had hitherto rejected, because the successful man she wanted

to marry had turned elsewhere? Its use of the theme of killing moles, its posing of the complex ties between love and cruelty, between love and death, between love and self-respect, between love and power—these are powerful achievements, though the story is slight enough, and everything is given full objective significance. Yet how full of Lawrence it is, in its imagery, its situation, its kind of sense of life: one can feel working in the story the rush of Lawrence's own experiences and preoccupations and beliefs. They work in *Kangaroo* more directly, sometimes more laxly, and the correlation between autobiography and fiction is often more clearly visible; but even in his most perfectly wrought works of fictional art—and they are to be found among his short stories—we can see the personal pattern and hear the beat of the Lawrentian passion.

In the short stories we feel that the action either contains what Lawrence wants to say, or it doesn't. There is rarely an approximation to success: the stories fail where the narrative is too crudely symbolic or where a meaning is imposed on the narrative by twists in the action or the dialogue that do not convince, and they succeed where the very texture of the narrative weaves as it moves the embodied meaning that Lawrence was seeking to communicate. Many of the stories, especially the earlier ones, are set in Lawrence's native Midland mining or farming country, and some of his most conspicuous successes show him maneuvering familiar kinds of incident into the pattern of meaning that he seeks. To do this he must combine the assured conviction of reality with a sense of the symbolic presentation of a meaning as almost simultaneous effects on the reader. One's first reaction to any good story must be to be convinced by it; yes, this was so and not otherwise. So that one is even tempted to say in reply to someone asking why did the author introduce *this* incident or present the character in *this* way, that this was how it happened, the author tells us this because it is clearly the truth; we ought to have this conviction conveyed to us by the whole movement and texture of the narrative. If we can answer such a question only by saying that the author wished to develop a certain idea or to introduce a certain kind of symbolism in the action, then we are either ignoring or denying his achievement as an artist. True, we can go on to demonstrate the symbolism or expound the idea, but the first response must be to the achieved reality of the story itself, and if we make no response to that, the implication is that it does not exist. In a sense, the critic is always at a loss before a fully realized work; he can only point to it and say "there, that's what I mean"; while the less successful work encourages him to separate action, idea, symbolism, and any other elements he wishes. So, with Joyce's *Ulysses*, the most immediate fact about the novel is that it is a world to be lived in, a real, multifaceted, human, functioning world; the symbolic patterns emerge only beyond this. And so, in *Daughters of the Vicar*, *You Touched Me*, *Samson and Delilah*, *The Horse Dealer's Daughter*, *Fanny and Annie*, *The Princess* (in its very different way), *The Blue Moccasins*, Lawrence, the very antithesis of Joyce as artist, projects situations which first of all compel *assent* and only after that convey their full charge of meaning.

Those short stories in which Lawrence imposes the meaning by an external device, as in *Glad Ghosts*, fall apart into the realized action and the imposed meaning, and this is true also (at least for this reader) of the often praised long short story or short novel, *The Ladybird*, where, in spite of some finely rendered incidents, the dialogue is often too explicitly charged with doctrine and the symbols too obviously im-

posed. Of the short novels, *The Fox* and *The Captain's Doll*
develop the symbolic expansion of meaning without strain
from the realized center of experience that is projected, even
more effectively than the popular *St. Mawr* where the horse
symbol is overinsistent and altogether too solemn. *Love
among the Haystacks*, the shortest of the long-short stories or
short novels, is another where the characters, environment,
and action coalesce immediately into a compellingly authentic world for the reader while at the same time the story
as told weaves patterns of meaning which transcend this
moment of life to embody truths about men and women and
the rhythms of love and work. The short story, *The Man
Who Loved Islands*, is in a different mode altogether; it is
fable told in a folk idiom, with just sufficient local particularization to prevent it from dissipating into abstraction.
Lawrence occasionally writes in this mode, but it is not
characteristic of him.

All these stories deal in one way or another with human
relationships, which remain always Lawrence's central
theme as a writer, but there is no monotony, for Lawrence
explores the theme from many different aspects and projects
it through many different kinds of narrative. The distortion
of love by possessiveness or gentility or a false romanticism
or a false conception of the life of art, and the achievement of
a living relation between a man and a woman in the teeth of
class feeling or tradition or habit or prejudice or even will—
these are bodied forth in the best of the stories with a
splendid actuality. Lawrence can present a whole rhythm of
life, a whole social tradition, through the account of one brief
incident securely localized in a pattern of thinking, feeling,
and behaving, as in *Odour of Chrysanthemums*, and at the
same time say something *critically* about human personality
and human relationships. The stories are all normative, but

the best ones only obliquely so; where he brings the norms
into the open in strident dialogue or melodramatic action
they are less persuasive, working less effectively in the story.
The Woman Who Rode Away, the story of an American
woman married to a Dutch-American settled in Mexico who
rides over the mountains to seek the old Indian religion in the
country of the Cilchuis and is accepted by them as a sacrifice
whose death will bring back the old gods, has the surface
bravura of so much of Lawrence's work set in Mexico, but it
also has a too obviously contrived symbolism of action and
the overexcited tone that Mexico seemed to produce in
Lawrence; beside it, the strength and reality of such stories
as *Fanny and Annie*, *Daughters of the Vicar*, and *The Fox*,
which are anchored in an English life that Lawrence knew
from the inside and where the meaning follows the "sense
of felt life" (in James's phrase), seem so much more impressive. Yet it would be a simplification to say that the stories of
Midland or in general of English life are always the best. *The
Prussian Officer* and *The Thorn in the Flesh*, both set in Ger-
many, are carefully wrought and highly charged stories introducing the factor of military discipline in its effect on human
consciousness and relationships, something with which
Lawrence never deals elsewhere. *The Rocking-Horse Winner*,
one of the best known of all Lawrence's stories, has power
and economy, but for all its very English setting it lacks a
dimension compared with those terribly English stories *The
Christening* or *Tickets Please* or some of those already mentioned.

Again in the short stories we sense the paradox of Lawrence the artist and Lawrence the compulsive improviser
working together, both helping each other and damaging each

other. The tone of genial laxness which enables him to end *The Primrose Path* with a perfunctory "And she did" is disconcerting in this instance, but it is an aspect of that same geniality (using the term in its earlier, Coleridgean sense) that led Lawrence to trust himself when writing, to trust to the impulse or the vision or the memory and the shape it took as he began to write. Though it is true that in such a novel as *The Rainbow* (as contrasted with *Kangaroo*) Lawrence worked over and perfected the shape with the greatest of care, it is also true that even in his most carefully revised writings he never eliminates the compulsive note that is part of his genius. It is not, therefore, that in some of his more hurried works art is lacking and mere autobiography takes control, while in his more finished productions everything is subordinated to the artistic pattern. It is rather that Lawrence's writing, both the good and the bad, both the revised and the impromptu, reflect his life in a rather special way, and all his work rises in some direct and one might almost say *necessary* manner from his own self, his committed and fighting self. The short stories, taken as a group, show very clearly how Lawrence's genius worked, how his fiction could be both relaxed and strenuous, both tentative and committed. The fierce discussion about Lawrence the man, which for at least two decades after his death took precedence over critical inquiry into the quality of his work, was, it might almost be said, inevitable, for the work postulates the man as the work of no other major English novelist does: even F. R. Leavis, who concentrates on Lawrence as artist and deplores Murry's judging of the work by the life, is led in his book on Lawrence to a variety of personal judgments on the nature and value of Lawrence's education, his relation to the England which produced him, and other extra-literary matters. One is led to quote again from Lawrence's Foreword to *Women in Love*: "The creative, spontaneous soul sends forth its promptings of desire and aspiration in us. These promptings are our true fate, which is our business to fulfil. . . . This novel pretends only to be a record of the writer's own desires, aspirations, struggles; in a word, a record of the profoundest experiences in the self." What is extraordinary is that even in a story of a lady's maid, thirty years old, coming reluctantly home to a provincial English town, after being jilted by the man she loved, to marry her second-best first love and to accept him even after discovering that a local girl had already had a child by him—even in such a story (*Fanny and Annie*), very Lawrentian in its plot, Lawrence conveys a sense of his own deepest self at work, of his own "creative, spontaneous soul" being involved.

Lawrence is a disturbing writer not in the obvious sense that in his less good work he makes the reader uncomfortable by his feverish overinsistence, though this is of course true; he is disturbing in the sense that in his best work he constantly forces the reader to question his own life. "If this is true—and it carries its own conviction—then what am I and what is my experience?" This is the sort of question that forms in the mind of the reader of Lawrence as he reads. You have to answer him, you have to come to terms with him. You cannot simply accept his vision of life as interesting or illuminating or aesthetically satisfying; you are compelled to apply it, to use it, to test it, to wonder about it. How utterly different this is from Joyce, who presents a world for our contemplation, a world to be enjoyed for its wholeness and patterned completeness, a world to be lived in for its fulness, not a world of challenging norms and provocative insights. Lawrence, like Blake, gets under the reader's skin with his radically new and personal view of experience, and like Blake he can outrage and exasperate. Like Blake, too, he faced a civilization whose basic values he flatly denied.

Joyce and Lawrence represent the two extremes of the modern novel. It has been argued that if you like one you cannot like the other, and it is certainly true that F. R. Leavis, Lawrence's greatest champion, despises Joyce's achievement. If you are Lawrence, you cannot admire Joyce, and Leavis writes entirely from Lawrence's point of view, as though he were himself Lawrence. But you need not be Lawrence, or write from his point of view, to see and admire his genius, any more than you need be committed to Joyce's view of the objectivity of the artist, who takes all views simultaneously and therefore takes no view, in order to appreciate Joyce. That is one advantage the critic has over certain kinds of creative artists: he can stand outside any given sort of commitment to experience or to art and appreciate it without himself being committed in that way. In a confused civilization where public standards of belief seem to be either declining or unreal the artist can stand outside all belief and with supreme yet humane objectivity see all possible values as equal provided life still goes on, and this is what Joyce did; or he can cultivate a fresh vision and try to present it in his art as a source of new value, which is what Lawrence did. He can also cultivate a fresh vision not as a source of new value but as a mode of personal sensibility, which is presented not as a curative vision for modern civilization but simply *as* a mode of personal sensibility: this is what Virginia Woolf did. Or, with an honest, exploratory pessimism, he can take elemental values where he can find them and test them out by showing what happens when the individual is challenged by circumstances to which those values do not seem to apply, and this is what Conrad did. Each attitude has proved artistically fruitful, yet each is in its own way highly personal, arising out of a personal response to a given phase of civilization, so that none of these four novelists has had the influence which their achievement might have led one to expect.

10

Virginia Woolf

In Virginia Woolf more than in any other English novelist the writer of fiction faces squarely the problem of the breakdown of a public sense of significance and its consequences for the novel. A novelist who could ask, "What is meant by reality?" and reply, "It would seem to be something very erratic, very undependable—now to be found in a dusty road, now in a scrap of newspaper in the street, now in a daffodil in the sun"; who specifically points out "the power of their belief" and the security of public conviction about fundamentals which distinguish Scott and Jane Austen from her own contemporaries—such a novelist does not have to wait for the critic to come along and explain what she is doing and why she is doing it. She saw one aspect of the modern problem with remarkable clarity, and consciously developed a view of fictional art which would enable her to deal with it. Of course she saw this not only as a modern problem but as a deep personal need—the need to develop a kind of fiction which would render persuasively the quality of her own personal insights into experience. "Quality" is the word to use here, for Mrs. Woolf was concerned less with projecting any given view of what is significant in experience than with the sort of thing, the moods, intuitions, blending of memories, sudden awarenesses of the symbolic in the real, that suggests how the inner life is really lived. The material environment, which she criticized Bennett and Wells and Galsworthy for concentrating on, was for her at most only a background, and even changes in status and fortune (where they occur in her novels, which is rarely) are shown as less interesting than the states of consciousness associated with them. Even the change from life to death can be less significant for her than the mutations of one person's consciousness into the differing recollections of that person, and the differing responses to the meaning of his or her personality, left in the consciousnesses of others after he or she has died. Mrs. Dalloway, reflecting on what death might mean, speculates that perhaps in death she would become "part of people she had never met; being laid out like a mist between the people she knew best, who lifted her on their branches as she had seen the trees lift the mist, but it spread ever so far, her life, herself." And in the last part of *To the Lighthouse* the dead Mrs. Ramsay is an important part of the texture of other consciousnesses.

It is true that in the rhythms of her prose, in the muted lilt of her sentences with their repetitions and qualifications and subtle fading from direct speech to brooding description and back again, Virginia Woolf sometimes provokes the reaction that it is all mere self-indulgent musing, an irresponsible playing about with life. But this is unjust. The novels are most carefully organized to present real patterns of meaning, and both characters and events are—by virtue of the way they are presented and of the part they play in the total pattern— endowed with symbolic significance that is much more than a mere sense of mood. Yet sense of mood is her starting point. The credibility of her best novels is established by the almost hypnotic force with which the author compels the reader to accept the mood she sets, with all its variations, as the novel flows on to its conclusion. Nothing could be further removed from Victorian fiction, in which the interest was maintained by public symbols, gain or loss of money, sudden fortune or sudden disgrace, or obvious emotional changes concerned with love or hate or hope or disappointment. The charge that Virginia Woolf's is an art of leisure, of unconcern with the practical affairs of daily life, is true but absurdly irrelevant. It might equally be made against the music of Mozart or the poems of Henry Vaughan. The important thing is that this delicate rendering of the different shades of experience, this subtle presentation of the texture of consciousness as it is woven by the individual's response to life, is made real and moving in Virginia Woolf's art. Whenever the claims of action are relaxed, whenever the pressure of external events is dropped so as to allow room for that leisure of the sensibilities in which the self can relish the meaning of its own responses and its own history, then Mrs. Woolf's world comes into existence. Perhaps the greatest fictional art weaves together the world of action and the world of introspection, the sense of the dailiness of daily living and the moods of private illumination which illumine and even transfigure routine; Virginia Woolf at her best restricts herself to certain kinds of response made possible in certain kinds of situation. She limited herself to this because it was this that interested her most and challenged her to produce her finest art. If we agree that her finest and most characteristic novels make their appeal to that twilight mood of receptive reverie (inducing that mood in the reader in order to appeal to it), if they steer us toward a new kind of knowledge through the rendering of almost familiar moods where we feel a deep sense of recognition and acquiescence and at the same time a sense of wonder and surprise; if they give us a general sense of meaning and relevance even before we have discovered what the meaning and relevance really are, that is all part of the intention. That, for Virginia Woolf, is how significance manifests itself in experience; she shows us her world of values in action, and in doing so makes use of our tendency to reverie—which is not the same as reducing all life to reverie. Thus while Joyce solves the problem of selection and significance by finding devices to enable him to show everything as simultaneously both significant and insignificant, Virginia Woolf, operating by restriction rather than by expansion, solves it by winning the co-operation of the reader's ordinary human tendency to reverie in order to present and to make convincing through a texture largely of reverie her own personal sense of significance. It may be true that she does not succeed in making her view convincing to all readers. A novelist who works by restriction in this way always risks limiting his appeal. But there will always be readers to whom her best and most characteristic novels will evoke that combination of recognition and discovery which only novels of real quality and originality can produce.

It is the texture of Virginia Woolf's novels which holds the reader, and the structure which determines the symbolic meanings of each phase of the action. This division of labor is more deliberate than it is in most novelists; in a sense it is artificial; but all art is artificial, and it is a matter of degree and of the convention within which an artist works. The large canvas, with its exuberant color and caricature, carrying the meaning along with careless splendor, is not Mrs. Woolf's way, though it is a way very deeply intrenched in the English literary tradition. Some readers resent having to hunt for the total meaning of a novel as they have to do for the meaning of a metaphysical poem. But this means that they have not been captured by the initial appeal of the texture, and if they have not there is nothing more to be said. To this extent Virginia Woolf is a minor novelist; one's response to her novels will depend in the last analysis on one's temperament. Some readers see her work as fantasy, charming in its way but essentially playful, and others see her as an aesthete who has refined life out of existence. Both views are wrong.

Fantasy is a legitimate enough literary form, but we can be fairly certain that none of Mrs. Woolf's novels, with the possible exception of *Orlando*, was written as fantasy. Virginia Woolf is interested in the life and problems of her time; she gives sufficient evidence of this in her non-fictional writing. In her novels she is endeavoring to present some essential truth about experience through the presentation of the contents of individual minds. She is not guilty of the heresy that by expressing herself she necessarily produces something of universal significance. She reaches out after life consciously, deliberately. "Perhaps without life nothing else is worth while," she has said herself in her essay on modern fiction. When we read many technically accomplished modern novels, she says, we recognize the craftsmanship: "but sometimes, more and more often as time goes by, we suspect a momentary doubt, a spasm of rebellion, as the pages fill themselves in the customary way. Is life like this? Must novels be like this?"[1] "Is life like this?" This is her criterion. There is no "art for art's sake" nonsense about Virginia Woolf; she recognizes the function of literature as that of illuminating experience for its readers. But where does one find experience? And how is it to be illuminated?

It is not only in the questions she poses but also in the man-

---

[1] Essay on "Modern Fiction," *The Common Reader* (1st ser., 1923).

ner in which she answers them that Mrs. Woolf displays the refining qualities of an aristocratic intellect. This is her answer:

> Examine for a moment an ordinary mind on an ordinary day. The mind receives a myriad impression—trivial, fantastic, evanescent, or engraved with the sharpness of steel. From all sides they come, an incessant shower of innumerable atoms; and as they fall, as they shape themselves into the life of Monday or Tuesday, the accent falls differently from of old; the moment of importance came not here but there; so that, if a writer were a free man and not a slave, if he could write what he chose, not what he must, if he could base his work upon his own feeling and not upon convention, there would be no plot, no comedy, no tragedy, no love interest or catastrophe in the accepted style, and perhaps not a single button sewn on as the Bond Street tailors would have it. Life is not a series of gig lamps symmetrically arranged; life is a luminous halo, a semi-transparent envelope surrounding us from the beginning of consciousness to the end. Is it not the task of the novelist to convey this varying, this unknown and uncircumscribed spirit, whatever aberration or complexity it may display, with as little mixture of the alien and external as possible?[2]

"Life is a luminous halo, a semi-transparent envelope surrounding us from the beginning of consciousness to the end." Life as it is objectively, that is to say, consists of that particular vision of life which certain sensitive beholders are blessed with. It is interesting that when faced with the problem of defining "real life" Mrs. Woolf asks her readers to look within. Katherine Mansfield asked rather for a clearer vision with which to look out. Yet the two procedures are not diametrically opposite, but tend rather to amount to very

---

[2] *Ibid.*

much the same thing. In practice, what it came to was this: Katherine Mansfield refined herself before looking out on life, while Virginia Woolf refined life before looking out on it. Katherine Mansfield regarded her preliminary personal refinement as a clarification of her vision; Virginia Woolf regarded her preliminary refinement of life as guaranteeing that she would concern herself only with what is important, true, or enduring. About the novels of Wells, Bennett, and Galsworthy, she says:

> If we fasten . . . one label on all these books, on which is one word materialists, we mean by it that they write of unimportant things; that they spend immense skill and immense industry making the trivial and the transitory appear the true and the enduring.[3]

But under what conditions can one man's sensibility judge between two rival views of truth and permanence in experience? A question we should like Mrs. Woolf to have answered for us.

So in Virginia Woolf we have one more novelist in whom a purely personal sense of significance replaces the sense of significance supplied by a tradition. The disintegration of the background of belief manifests itself in many interesting ways. To accept the traditional schematization was unartistic to Joyce, meant the lack of objective truth to Katherine Mansfield, and meant the presentation of the unimportant and the trivial to Virginia Woolf.

It is rarely that an artist is conscious of the forces in civilization that are compelling him to write as he does. The artistic mind tends to think in terms of absolutes and universal laws: there have been few if any leaders of new move-

---

[3] *Ibid.*

ments in art who were aware of what conditioned their view
or who regarded their movement only as a temporary ex-
pedient for meeting a transient situation. But Mrs. Woolf laid
her finger on one of the main conditioning factors of her attitude and technique:

> To believe that your impressions hold good for others is to
> be released from the cramp and confinement of personality.
> It is to be free, as Scott was free, to explore with a vigour
> which still holds us spell-bound the whole world of adventure
> and romance. It is also the first step in that mysterious process
> in which Jane Austen was so great an adept. The little grain
> of experience once selected, believed in, and set outside her-
> self, could be put precisely in its place, and she was then free
> to make it . . . into that complete statement which is litera-
> ture.
>
> So then our contemporaries afflict us because they have
> ceased to believe. The most sincere of them will only tell us
> what it is that happens to himself. They cannot make a world,
> because they are not free of other human beings.[4]

It is a matter of belief. Your own impressions hold good for
others if both you and your public accept automatically a
common schematization of reality, but not otherwise. That
was why Scott and Jane Austen enjoyed the freedom Mrs.
Woolf describes. That is why "our contemporaries afflict us
because they have ceased to believe." This is precisely the
problem of a transition period that we have tried to indicate
in earlier chapters. Mrs. Woolf's attitude and technique
represent one attempt to solve that problem: it is under-
standable that she should have thought it the only possible
one.

Mrs. Woolf's particular kind of refinement of life led
eventually to the emergence of one theme which dominates

---

[4] "How It Strikes a Contemporary," *ibid.*

all her fiction, from *Mrs. Dalloway* to *The Years.* This is a theme characteristically abstract, characteristically philosophical, to which action, character, and commentary are alike subordinated; the theme of time, death, and personality and the relations of these three to each other and to some ultimate which includes them all. Significance in events is increasingly judged in terms of these three factors. It is not so much the quality of the observation of life (as it is in Katherine Mansfield) which makes her points, but reflection after observation. A twofold process of rarification goes on. First, life is refined before it is observed with the artist's eye; second, the results of observation are meditatively chewed on as they are being presented to the reader. A certain lack of body in her work is the result.

Mrs. Woolf began her career as a novelist with the publication of *The Voyage Out* in 1915. It is a slow and rather dull piece of work, traditional in style and conventionally ambitious in scope. It is, in fact, the promising first novel—but with a difference. The plot is quiet, with no complications and no moments of high tension, no usual feature of the promising first novel. There is a quiet impressionism in the telling of the story which deals with the development of Rachel Vinrace from the time when she sails on the voyage out with the other characters on the "Euphrosyne" up to her peaceful death in the hospital at Santa Marina just after she has acquired the ability to take a grip on life. Already we see what is to be a characteristic theme of the author's—death as a part of life, an incident in life, and a means to its interpretation. Throughout the book a highly rarefied life flows gently on, the individuals merging gracefully into the stream. Death is an incident, and the stream flows on. There is a suggestion that reality is, in a sense, outside time—a suggestion that we are to meet with again and again in Virginia Woolf's work. The escape from chronology is a common and significant feature of modern fiction: when life as a series of chronological events ceases to have meaning, every possible new way of re-creating value is explored.

Night and Day (1919) demonstrated to Mrs. Woolf herself that the disparity between her matter and her manner was threatening her with inhibition as a novelist altogether. You cannot distil refined essences of time and personality while employing the traditional technique of the novel. The kind of novel form Mrs. Woolf had up till now been using had been evolved over a period of well over a century as the best means of presenting a pattern of significant events. But Mrs. Woolf wanted to present a distillation of significant ideas about events, which was a very different thing, and required a much less rigid form. This is not the "novel of ideas," which is a very much older form, but a much more tenuous thing—the novel of refined lyrical speculation. In *Night and Day* Mrs. Woolf makes her last attempt to use the traditional novel form for her increasingly untraditional purposes. But she is caught in its toils. And the more she struggles the more she becomes enmeshed, until the novel becomes the very opposite, we suspect, of what it was intended to be—a heavy, protracted piece of work with a quite glaring disparity between form and content. As though to compensate, the characters are made to indulge desperately in long monologues, trying to break down the restricting barriers of fact and event, trying to win through to the freer realms of meditative lyricism which Mrs. Woolf achieved in *Mrs. Dalloway* and, most successfully of all, in parts of *To the Lighthouse*. Katherine, the heroine, with her fierce desire to be honest with herself and her many intellectual qualities (we catch many glimpses of her creator) drags her way slowly through the book, proceeding from action to speculation and from speculation to action in a manner which finally wearies the reader. We can see now that what Virginia Woolf required was a technique which would unite action and speculation in one "semi-transparent envelope."

Night and Day has many impressive qualities. The individual chracters are carefully studied and presented; the psychological aspect of the novel is seriously and thoughtfully done; many of the critical incidents are presented with vividness and power. But the traditional form of patterned external action illustrating or corresponding to the relevant ideas of the author is too rigid to contain successfully what Mrs. Woolf had to say. When fiction is part of a stable and confident civilization, such a technique becomes the natural one; but a sensitive and original artist of Mrs. Woolf's generation, with her heredity, her problems, her desire to emancipate herself from a background which she believed to be far more rigid than the nature of things warranted—such a writer would soon be forced to realize the inadequacy of that technique and to search for a new one.

It was not a long search. It is represented in a little volume published in 1921 under the title *Monday or Tuesday*. Here the no man's land between prose and poetry, between fiction and lyricism, is carefully explored. Here all the traditional features of prose narrative—plot, characterization, description, etc.—are deliberately blurred into a new unity, into a "luminous halo, a semi-transparent envelope." Sensibility is sent wandering to and fro, noting this, lingering on that, collecting facts, impressions, moods, ideas, uniting them all into that diaphanous whole which for Mrs. Woolf is the true symbol of life. Some of the sketches in this volume are simply studies in impressionism. "The String Quartet" and "The Haunted House" are little more than this. But even here it is not impressionism for its own sake that Mrs. Woolf is giving us, but an exploration of the possibilities of certain types of impressionist approach—their possibilities for novel-writing, for helping to create the feel of life as she understood it. Sketches like "The Mark on the Wall" and "Kew Gardens" explore the subtler aspects of the relation between the senses and the emotions, between physical and mental experience; we see, for example, a certain color effect suggesting certain ideas which in turn suggest certain effects in terms of one of the other senses. The mind, or perhaps more accurately the sensibility, is a kind of general junction; something enters as a sense perception and emerges as a thought or a mood or another kind of sense perception. And around the whole lies the semitransparent envelope. The whole purpose of these experiments is most adequately illustrated by the title sketch, "Monday or Tuesday," where we see clearly the attempt to create a distilled essence of reality by combining in a unity, whose context is more poetical or lyrical than fictional, a host of sense impressions, records of fact, and speculations. What larger purpose this new technique is to serve is not altogether clear from *Monday or Tuesday*, although in the light of her subsequent work it is not difficult to find its microcosm in this book of sketches. One thing, however, could have been predicted with certainty by the first reviewer of the book: henceforth, Mrs. Woolf had cast the traditional technique behind her and was to use it no more.

In her essay on "Modern Fiction," from which we have already quoted, Virginia Woolf referred with approval to Joyce's *Ulysses*, then (1919) appearing in the *Little Review*. There were many aspects of the technique of *Ulysses* that must have appealed to her. The "stream of consciousness" method, so useful in breaking down the distinction between subject and object and in suggesting rather than describing states of mind, must have impressed her in Joyce and in Dorothy Richardson (five parts of whose *Pilgrimage* had already appeared). For breaking down distinctions and suggesting rather than stating were two important ways of creating the "luminous halo, [the] semi-transparent envelope surrounding us from the beginning of consciousness to the end." Already in 1919 Virginia Woolf was contrasting Joyce with the other English novelists of her time:

> In contrast with those whom we have called materialists Mr. Joyce is spiritual; he is concerned at all costs to reveal the flickerings of that innermost flame which flashes its messages through the brain, and in order to preserve it he disregards with complete courage whatever seems to him adventitious, whether it be probability, or coherence or any other of these signposts which for generations have served to support the imagination of a reader when called upon to imagine what he can neither touch nor see.[5]

It is interesting to see Mrs. Woolf discussing Joyce's technique in terms of her own purpose. Their purposes were in fact very different. Joyce's aim was to isolate reality from all human attitudes—an attempt to remove the normative element from fiction completely, to create a self-contained world independent of all values in the observer, independent even (as though this were possible) of all values in the creator. But Virginia Woolf refines on values rather than eliminates them. Her reaction to crumbling norms is not agnosticism but sophistication. It might be argued that a meditative refinement of experience, of the kind that Mrs. Woolf gives us

---

[5] "Modern Fiction," *ibid.*

in *To the Lighthouse* or *Mrs. Dalloway*, is halfway to the vacuum world of Joyce, because the ultimate point of refinement comes when we refine out of existence. From the rarefied atmosphere of *To the Lighthouse* to the completely neutral atmosphere of *Ulysses* is perhaps but a step. Such an argument would at least have the merit of recognizing a common object in the work of these two writers, namely, escape from the necessity of utilizing a value framework which they both recognized, consciously or unconsciously, to have crumbled. A sufficiently rarified philosophy is, for all practical purposes, very close to complete unbelief. But it is not complete unbelief, and therefore Mrs. Woolf does not have Joyce's problem, which is to present to the reader a world for contemplation without believing, or implying any belief, that that world is worth contemplating. Joyce's colossal technical virtuosity is a way of hiding that problem from himself, just as the slogan "art for art's sake" is a way of disguising a belief in the worthlessness of art which, if expressed bluntly, would be too discouraging for the artist. So if the immediate purposes of James Joyce and Virginia Woolf were very different, their ultimate purposes were perhaps the same—to find a solution to the all-important value problem. Joyce went the whole way in rejecting the normative and involved himself in an immense paradox; Virginia Woolf went only halfway (probably without being conscious that she was going in that direction at all) and stopped at subtilization. When she calls Wells, Bennett, and Galsworthy "materialists," what she really means is that they accept the old, traditional criteria in describing events, while she is conscious of the dissolution of those criteria. The issue does not really lie between materialists and idealists, but between those who accept and those who reject the traditional norms in discussing experience. When Virginia Woolf said that "Mr. Joyce is spiritual," she meant that Mr. Joyce had shown himself, by his method of writing, to be dissatisfied with those norms. If in her own case such dissatisfaction was to result in spiritualization of experience, in mediative refinement of events, that did not mean that spiritualization was the only way out.

But whatever the precise relation of Joyce's work to that of Mrs. Woolf, the fact remains that after *Monday or Tuesday* Mrs. Woolf was committed to the search for a new method in the organization and presentation of narrative which arose from the necessity of finding a method of treating experience which, while normative, was yet liberated from the traditional schematization. To seek for such liberation and yet desire to retain value criteria is a very delicate task, and perhaps this explains why Mrs. Woolf achieved her state of unstable equilibrium only two or three times in her career as a novelist. It is, however, a task which does not raise the even greater problems which await those who, like Joyce, profess to believe in experience without distinguishing values within it.

Jacob's Room appeared in 1922, and here we see Virginia Woolf deliberately experimental both in theme and in technique. The theme is to become her favorite one: the nature of personality and its relation to time and death. Jacob, the hero, is presented, not directly through description, but through the impressions which are relevant to his personality. Thus we are shown what he sees and what is to be seen in his environment; the reflection of him in other persons' minds; what he himself thinks, feels, does (but little of the last); what is felt and thought by others who move in his world; and, finally, what impressions which originally took their origin in his personality remain with others after his death. Jacob's character emanates, as it were, from the book; Virginia Woolf's technique is deliberately by indirections to find directions out. Jacob's room is used as an integrating factor, though not so consistently as the title might lead us to believe. The atmosphere of the whole book is tenuous, largely because the author's aim is speculative rather than descriptive. The question implicitly posed by the story—if story it can be called—is in essence a metaphysical rather than a psychological one; and the answer is not stated but suggested. What is personality? How does it impinge on its environment? What is its relation to events in time? What is the nature of reality in so far as it is related to the mental and emotional world of men? It is to answer these questions that Virginia Woolf selects and refines on data abstracted with care and delicacy from human experience.

The aeration of her style which was one of the many ways in which Mrs. Woolf tried to free herself from the inhibiting features of the traditional novel—an aeration which *Night and Day* showed her to be much in need of, and which is shown in process in *Monday or Tuesday*—was perhaps carried a little too far in *Jacob's Room*, and in her following novel, *Mrs. Dalloway* (1925), there is a successful attempt to redress the balance. By this time the "stream of consciousness" technique had become almost a commonplace in fiction, and the problem was not so much to win freedom to employ it as to find a way of disciplining it. It is one thing to have the relation between your characters' impressions clear in your own mind and quite another to have them objectively clear in the form of the work itself. Virginia Woolf seems to have grappled carefully with the latter problem in *Mrs. Dalloway:* she limits its scope in time and place; her characters are few and their relations to each other clear-cut; impressions and thought processes are assigned clearly to those to whom they belong, even at the risk of losing some immediacy of effect; the time scheme is patterned with extraordinary care; and altogether the novel represents as neat a piece of construction as she has ever achieved. It is therefore an excellent example to take for a more detailed technical analysis.

Just as Joyce in *Ulysses* takes one day in the life of Leopold Bloom and enlarges its implications by patterning its events with sufficient care, so Virginia Woolf takes from morning to evening in the life of Mrs. Dalloway and builds her story through the events of this short time. (Events, of course, include psychological as well as physical happenings.) Being a far shorter and less ambitious work than *Ulysses*, *Mrs. Dalloway* employs a simpler and more easily analyzable technique. The whole novel is constructed in terms of the two dimensions of space and time. We either stand still in time and are led to contemplate diverse but contemporaneous events in space or we stand still in space and are allowed to move up and down temporally in the consciousness of one individual. If it would not be extravagant to consider personality rather than space as one dimension, with time as the other, we might divide the book quite easily into those sections where time is fluid and personality stable or where personality is fluid and time is stable, and regard this as a careful alternation of the dimensions. So that at one point we are halted at a London street to take a peep into the consciousness of a variety of people who are all on the spot at the same moment in the same place, and at another we are halted within the consciousness of one individual moving up and down in time within the limits of one individual's memory. The two methods might be represented diagrammatically as shown on page 204.

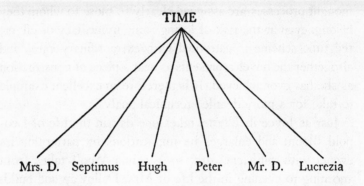

TIME

Mrs. D.   Septimus   Hugh   Peter   Mr. D.   Lucrezia

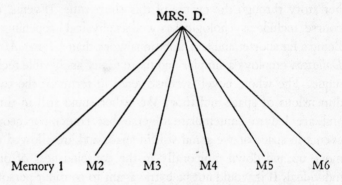

MRS. D.

Memory 1   M2   M3   M4   M5   M6

In the first case time is the unifying factor, making, without the knowledge of anyone except the omniscient author, significant patterns out of chance. (But, Is it chance? and What is chance? Mrs. Woolf would ask.)

Here personality is the unifying factor, seeking a pattern in time by means of memory. Taking A, B, C, etc., to represent characters, T to represent the present moment (in terms of the action of the novel) and T_1, T_2, T_3, etc., to represent past moments, we might diagrammatically represent the movement of the novel as a whole as shown on page 205.

The groups of T's are, of course, different, as being presented through the consciousness of different characters.

And the book does not proceed in the straightforward mathematical way indicated by the diagrams; but that is its general movement. The plot is carried forward through the line ATFTATBTA, beginning and ending with the principal character on the day whose action is described. Of course, T in the diagram is not a unique moment of time, but simply any moment of the day in question; actually, T progresses

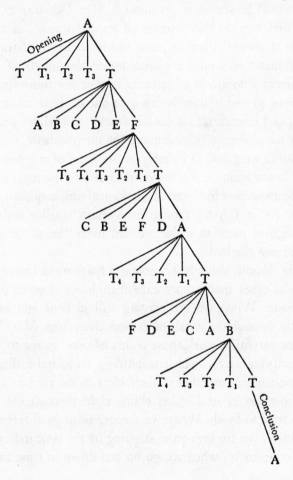

from morning to night through each stage in the diagram. The fact that the line ATFTATBTA, though it represents the carrying-forward of the chrolonogical action (the plot, in the vulgar sense), represents only discrete fragments of thought and action and gives no adequate view of the real story is partly the measure of Mrs. Woolf's deviation from traditional methods in her construction of the story.

It would be simple to go through *Mrs. Dalloway* to show how first we get the "stream of consciousness" of a particular character; then we pause to look over the character's environment and take a glance inside the minds of other characters who are in or relevant to that environment; then we come to rest within the mind of one of those other characters and investigate his consciousness for a while; and then again we emerge to contemplate the environment, etc. And each time we pause to investigate the mind of any one character in some detail, that mind takes us into the past, and we escape altogether from the chronological time sequence of the story. As in *Ulysses*, though on a much smaller scale, the past figures more than the present, even though the action covers one single day.

Mrs. Woolf, although her scope is much more limited than Joyce's, takes much more care than Joyce does to put up signposts. When we are staying still in time and moving rapidly through the minds of various characters, Mrs. Woolf is very careful to mark those points of time, to see to it that the unifying factor which is holding these quite disparate consciousnesses together is made clear to the reader. That is why the clocks of London chime right through the book, from start to finish. When we wander through different personalities, we are kept from straying by the time indications, and, conversely, when we go up and down in time through the memory of one of the characters, we are kept from straying by the constant reminder of the speaker's identity. There is nothing haphazard about the striking of the clocks:

> "The time, Septimus," Rezia repeated. "What is the time?"
> He was talking, he was starting, this man must notice him. He was looking at them.
> "I will tell you the time," said Septimus, very slowly, very drowsily, smiling mysteriously. As he sat smiling at the dead man in the grey suit the quarter struck—the quarter to twelve.
> And that is being young, Peter Walsh thought as he passed them.

We pass from Septimus Smith to Peter Walsh, and the striking of the hour marks the transition. If we are not to lose our way among the various consciousnesses, we must understand why we are taken from one to another: because they impinge in time, and that impingement is symbolized by the striking of the clock. Almost every fifteen minutes is indicated by a clock chiming, or in some other way, throughout the book. We can always find out, at most by looking a page ahead or consulting the previous page, just what time of day it is. And these indications of time are most clearly given when we are about to go from personality to personality— through one of the ABCD rather than the $T_1 T_2 T_3$ lines.

Similarly, when we pause within the consciousness of one character only to move up and down in time within that consciousness, the identity of the thinker, which this time is the unifying factor, is stressed. The opening paragraphs provide a characteristic example:

> Mrs. Dalloway said she would buy the flowers herself.
> For Lucy had her work cut out for her. The doors would be taken off their hinges; Rumpelmayer's men were coming. And then, thought Clarissa Dalloway, what a morning— fresh as if issued to children on a beach.

What a lark! What a plunge! For so it had always seemed to her, when, with a little squeak of the hinges, which she could hear now, she had burst open the French windows and plunged at Bourton into the open air. How fresh, how calm, stiller than this of course, the air was in the early morning; like the flap of a wave; the kiss of a wave; chill and sharp and yet (for a girl of eighteen as she then was) solemn, feeling as she did, standing there at the open window, that something awful was about to happen. . . .

The compromise between reported and direct thought here seems to be due to Mrs. Woolf's desire to keep the unifying factor always present to the reader's mind, but it has some interesting results. The "I" of the reverie becomes an indeterminate kind of pronoun midway between "she" (which it would have been had Mrs. Woolf used the straight objective reporting of the traditional novel) and the first personal pronoun employed naturally by the real "stream of consciousness" writer. It is not surprising to find Mrs. Woolf frequently taking refuge in "one," as in the following very characteristic sentence: "For having lived in Westminster—how many years now? over twenty—one feels even in the midst of the traffic, or waking at night, Clarissa was positive, a particular hush, or solemnity. . . ."

Here the movement is from a suppressed "I" (in the parenthetical clause) to a "one" and then, on account of the necessity of stressing the unifying factor, namely the identity of Clarissa Dalloway, to a straight third-person use of "Clarissa." We might note, too, the frequent use of the present participle (". . . she cried to herself, pushing through the swing doors"; "she thought, waiting to cross," ". . . she asked herself, walking towards Bond Street"), which enables her to identify the thinker and carry her into a new action without interrupting the even flow of the thought stream; and the frequent commencement of a paragraph with "for," the author's conjunction (not the thinker's), whose purpose is to indicate the vague, pseudo-logical connection between the different sections of a reverie.

The plot in *Mrs. Dalloway* is made to act out the meaning of the reverie in a most interesting manner. As the heroine reflects on the nature of the self and its relation to other people, on the importance of contact and at the same time the necessity of keeping the self inviolable, of the extremes of isolation and domination, other characters in London at the same time—some encountered by and known to Mrs. Dalloway, and others quite unknown to her—illustrate in their behavior, thoughts, relations to each other, and so on, different aspects of these problems. Hugh Whitbread, whom she meets early in her morning shopping, is the perfect social man, handsome, well-bred, "with his little job at Court," who has almost lost his real personality in fulfilling his social function; though, Mrs. Dalloway reflects, he is "not a positive imbecile as Peter made out; not a mere barber's block," there is an element of glossy unreality about him. It is significant that at this stage Peter Walsh should come into Mrs. Dalloway's mind, for Peter (the man she had loved and who had loved her but whom she had refused to marry because he made too many claims on her individuality and wished to dominate her personality with his own) is at the other extreme, the individual who never really adjusts to society; he stands in some ways for the independent and assertive self, all the more vulnerable for its independence. Later on in the novel he turns up at Mrs. Dalloway's (having conveniently just returned from India) and is invited to her party that evening, where he takes his place both as part of the pattern of Mrs. Dalloway's past and as a particular kind of sensibility recording appropriate impressions. The delicate working-out of differing degrees of selfhood and social adjustment can be compared and contrasted with the same sort of thing as it is done by a great novelist working in an assured social world through public symbols. In Jane Austen's *Pride and Prejudice* we are also shown differing degrees of selfhood and of adjustment, but the degrees have moral implications and there is an ideal adjustment in which morality as well as happiness resides. Elizabeth Bennet, who at first depends too impulsively on personal impressions and personal desires, learns to modify her individualism in response to the demands of the social world of other people, while Darcy, who at first leans too much on his place in society, learns to modify his social pride and to trust also the claims of individuality: flanking each of them at the extremes of immoral absurdity is the self-indulgent individualism of Lydia and the preposterous snobbery of Lady Catherine de Brough. Such a moral pattern, depending on the belief (shared with her readers) that an ideal adjustment between self and society was both desirable and possible, was unavailable to Virginia Woolf, who sees the problem as psychological rather than as moral.

Nevertheless there are moral implications, of a much more personal kind, in *Mrs. Dalloway*. Septimus Warren Smith, whose experience in the war has led him to a state of mind in which he cannot respond at all to the reality of the existence of other people, is driven mad by this meaningless isolation of the self, and his madness is exacerbated into suicide by the hearty doctors who insist that all he has to do is to imitate the public gestures of society (eat porridge for breakfast and play golf) and he will become an integrated character again. That this ideal of integration is mechanical and false is made clear by the picture of Lady Bradshaw (the wife of the specialist whose visit drives Septimus to his death) as a creature bullied into nothingness by the public face of her husband. And, even more significantly, Virginia Woolf brings the Bradshaws to Mrs. Dalloway's party that evening, and when Sir William Bradshaw tells her of the young man who had committed suicide that afternoon, Mrs. Dalloway feels a pang of sympathy and understanding for the victim and a revulsion against Sir William. She sees Sir William as "obscurely evil," "extremely polite to women, but capable of some indescribable outrage—forcing your soul, that was it"; and she sees herself for a moment as the doomed young man, associating his death with themes in her own meditations that have already been traced throughout the novel. At the same time as this kind of plot-weaving is going on, we are also shown characters and actions who weave a pattern of the moment and the flux, the self standing like an upright sword amid the waters of the time and the flow of consciousness and the world of other selves. Mrs. Dalloway watches through her window an old lady in the house opposite getting ready for bed, and as she looks at her through glass this becomes a symbol of how we are related to others—through an invisible glass wall (a device used more conspicuously in *To the Lighthouse*). The old lady puts her light out and goes to bed, and contact is lost. Mrs. Dalloway returns to the party, and as she reappears Peter Walsh is seized by "extraordinary excitement." The reality of Mrs. Dalloway's personality, her actual presence at that time and place, suddenly overwhelms him:

> It is Clarissa, he said.
> For there she was.

That is how the novel ends, with the emphasis on identity. But this is not a solution, or a resolution; it is simply a phase of an endless pattern of which the elements are personality, consciousness, time, relationship, and the basic theme, the relation of loneliness to love.

The above remarks are not meant to constitute an analysis of *Mrs. Dalloway*, which would require a long chapter to itself, but only an indication of how Virginia Woolf builds up her characteristic kind of novel. It should be added that in spite of the meditative refinement that goes on throughout the book we are also given a vivid sense of London in the early 1920's: the social scene—although its relevance for the individual remains problematical—is set with greater concreteness and brilliance than it is in any other of her more successful novels. We may feel that the refining intellect is mocked by the sheer actuality of the city bustle which is presented so effectively, but that feeling is at times shared by the heroine herself. The flux and the moment, the individual and his social environment, were constantly challenging each other. "In people's eyes, in the swing, tramp, and trudge; in the bellow and the uproar; the carriages, motor cars, omnibuses, vans, sandwich men shuffling and swinging; brass bands; barrel organs; in the triumph and the jingle and the strange high singing of some aeroplane overhead was what she loved; life; London; this moment of June."

In *To the Lighthouse*, published in 1927, Mrs. Woolf avoids any risk of having a substantial urban world challenge the reality of the subtle reveries of the characters. She compromises between her refining intellect and the real external world by limiting her definition of the real to its refinable aspects and at the same time recognizing the definition as a limited one. The setting, in northwest Scotland, is not only appropriate to the half-lyrical mood in which the book is written, but it is also an adequate symbol of those aspects of action and emotion in which she is most interested and which she is best able to handle. The time-death-personality theme is handled much more explicitly than in the earlier novels, and with real success. The rarefied atmosphere for the first time is right; it corresponds adequately to the situation. This is minor fiction at its most triumphant—minor, because after all it does deal with a backwater of human experience; triumphant, because it is done so perfectly. In terms of diurnal reviewing, to call a work minor might imply the height of abuse, but it is not in that sense that the term is here used. A first-rate minor work is worth many second-rate major ones.

There are some interesting differences in technique between *Mrs. Dalloway* and *To the Lighthouse*. In the latter book the time scheme is wider and mood and retrospect are shown against a background of actual change, not only remembered change as in the former. In the first part of *To the Lighthouse* the reader is presented with what the characters look back on in the last part, and this leaves the author freer than she was in *Mrs. Dalloway* in her weaving of musing and recollection. There is no need to be so careful about signposts. The wider freedom in *To the Lighthouse* is the direct result of the greater limitation of the world presented. If you limit your world to a circumscribed area within which everything is relevant to the pattern your wish to weave, you are freer to move where you will in that world than you would be if you chose a larger world and wove your pattern by means of rigid selection and abstraction. That is the difference between the two novels.

To the Lighthouse represents that state of unstable equilibrium which most really good minor artists achieve but once in their careers. Everything conspires to minimize the author's characteristic defects. Virginia Woolf's tendency for making everything transparent, including the most solid things of life, is most happily employed when it works on a collection of intellectuals set down at holiday time in the Isle of Skye. Perhaps the author realized this, for her next work, *Orlando*, published in 1928, is a deliberate attempt to express some of her main themes through fantasy. It is a threefold stage: First, there is the attempt to create an abstract pattern by unduly refining on the events of the real world; then comes a restriction of the real world to those aspects which can stand such refinement with least distortion; finally, the real world is left behind, to be drawn on or ignored at will, and the abstract pattern has no responsibility to life at all.

Orlando is a brilliant *jeu d'esprit* rather than a serious novel. Tracing the physical and literary ancestors of her friend, Victoria Sackville West, from late Elizabethan times to the present, through the adventures of a hero who changes sex en route and treating that hero as nevertheless a single personality, Mrs. Woolf manages to collect on her way some highly effective descriptions of scenes partly historical and partly imaginary, displaying a colorfulness and a vivacity that the rest of her fiction conspicuously lacks. It is perhaps illuminating that the most vivacious of her books should be the most fantastic and in many ways the least serious. In spite of the element of fantasy, in spite of the irresponsible hero who marches through time from one impossible situation to another, the book has tremendous vigor and pulses with life. The earlier portions particularly, when the hero is still in the seventeenth century, have a reality that poor Mrs. Dalloway never attained. Probably no two novelists were ever more dissimilar than Virginia Woolf and Eric Linklater, but there is a smack of Linklater in *Orlando*, which certainly adds to the book's qualities. It would be a weary task to disentangle the profoundly symbolic from the deliberately irresponsible in *Orlando:* it is a book to be read with the surface of the mind and enjoyed for its surface brilliance. It would be unfair to its author and to its readers to treat it as a great novel.

The Waves, published in 1931, displays more conscious virtuosity than any other of Virginia Woolf's novels. There is a more concentrated use of symbolism, a more deliberate employment of set prose rhythms, and in general the work is more like a prose poem than a novel. Time divisions in the lives of the six characters are marked by set descriptions of seascapes at different periods of the day, and the characters speak throughout in stylized monologues through which their natures, their attitudes, and the story of their lives from infancy to death are presented. Again, time, death, and personality, and their interrelations, provide the main theme; here, the emphasis is on time. The continuous use of the formal interior monologue indicates the high degree of artifice employed in the book. It contains some beautiful prose, some sensitive and suggestive writing, and a carefully woven pattern of meaning, but the level of stylization results in a certain lack of vitality; if the work is a novel, we demand more of what James called "the sense of felt life" than this technique can achieve; and if it is not a novel, there should surely be a more lyrical concentration of meaning than this long sequence of monologues can achieve. Not that one wishes to impose on Virginia Woolf any external criterion of "the novel," but one does demand that a work of literary art should achieve its own form by the most appropriate devices. *The Waves* is a book to be admired; in some ways it shows more virtuosity than anything else its author wrote; but it does not live in the imagination of readers as the two preceding novels do.

The Years (1937) seems at first sight to be a return to the method of *Night and Day;* it moves through time in a more conventional manner and tells the life histories of the main characters in steady chronological sequence. But there is a difference. The prose is more weighted with meaning, more fraught with luminous flashes of suggestion and symbolization, than in the early novel. Virginia Woolf herself, writing of *The Years* in her diary when she was just beginning it (its original title was to be *The Pargiters*), called it an "Essay-Novel" and remarked that "it's to take in everything, sex, education, life etc.: and come, with the most powerful and agile leaps, like a chamois, across precipices from 1880 to here and now." This sounds very old-fashioned, and indeed one cannot help feeling that in this novel the author's characteristic subtlety and suggestiveness of style are wasted when the plot itself is extended at such length and packed with so many incidents and references. Mrs. Woolf rewrote it several times, each time trying to sharpen and compress, but it still remains a novel where the meaning is achieved by *depth* while the form demands a meaning achieved largely by *extension*, and the result is not altogether convincing. "In this book I have discovered that there must be contrast," she wrote in her diary; "one strata [*sic*] or layer can't be developed intensively, as I did I expect in *The Waves,* without harm to others." One can understand why she felt the need to move away from the high stylization of *The Waves,* but at the same time one feels that she went too far in the other direction. Her delicate art demanded a very precarious unstable equilibrium, and it was all too easy to fall over on one side or the other.

In her last book, *Between the Acts* (1941), Virginia Woolf returned to the method that best suited her genius. This story of a pageant of English history, presented in an English village on a June day in 1939, uses both the sensibilities of the principal characters and the words spoken at the pageant by the actors as means of concentrating meaning in an interpretation of the English past and its relation to the present and of the relation of individuals to history. It is done with a finely achieved lyrical feeling, which is so persuasively accounted for in the characters and the action that the reader feels no sense of overstylization as he might in reading *The Waves*. There are moments in the novel when the technique is almost that of symbolist poetry; but the poetic devices never get out of control and the total pattern of meaning emerges cumulatively as this most delicately wrought work unfolds itself. Between the acts of the pageant of English history, minor personal dramas of characters and groups of characters are played out; the cross-patterning of individual and community, of present and past, of retrospect and anticipation, of isolation and communication, is achieved by the deft use of correspondences between different levels of the book's action; and the personality and poetic fancy of one of the chief characters, Isa Oliver, not only makes probable in terms of the action the modulation into highly charged lyrical prose but also interweaves with the imagination of the author of the pageant, Miss La Trobe, the outsider who is in some respects the type of the artist struggling to communicate a private vision through a public medium. The actual narrative is carried on by a prose so finely adjusted that it allows equally for development into a lyrical, symbolic use of language and for the less intensive function of carrying on the framework of the story. The unstable equilibrium which Virginia Woolf's art demanded is here perfectly achieved.

Index